Workbook

American Red Cross
Child Care Course
Child Development Units

Produced in cooperation with

American Academy
of Pediatrics

98 99 00 01 02 / 9 8 7 6

ISBN: 0-86536-184-3

Acknowledgments

Members of the American Red Cross Child Care Course instructional design and development team included Jessica Bernstein, M.P.H.; Robert Dirmeyer; Iris Graham; Alexandra G. Greeley; Cindy Green, M.P.H.; Carol Hunter-Geboy, Ph.D.; Alice D. Lowe; Pamela B. Mangu, M.A.; Lynda Ramsey; and Bruce Spitz. Assistance was provided by Jeanne P. Luschin, M.B.A.; Lawrence D. Newell, Ed.D.; Cynthia Vlasich, R.N.; S. Elizabeth White, M.A.Ed.; and the Office of Health and Safety Operations.

Special technical assistance was provided by Susan Aronson, M.D., F.A.A.P., Hahnemann University.

Technical advice was provided by:
Jeanie Snodgrass Almo, R.N., M.S.N.

Robert G. Bruce, Ph.D.

Valerie Williams Drake, M.A.

Patricia D. Fosarelli, M.D., The Johns Hopkins Children's Center

Andrea Carlson Gielen, Sc.D., The Johns Hopkins University School of Hygiene and Public Health

Murray L. Katcher, M.D., Ph.D., State of Wisconsin Division of Health

Janet Brown McCracken, M.Ed.

Andrew McGuire, The Trauma Foundation at San Francisco General Hospital

Suzanne M. Randolph, Ph.D., University of Maryland

Patricia Riley, C.N.M., M.P.H., U.S. Public Health Service

Frederick Rivara, M.D., University of Washington

Anita Sandretto, M.P.H., The University of Michigan School of Public Health

RoseAnn Soloway, R.N., M.S.Ed., C.S.P.I., National Capital Poison Center, Georgetown University Hospital

John A. Steward, R.S., M.P.H., Centers for Disease Control

Stephen Teret, J.D., M.P.H., The Johns Hopkins University School of Hygiene and Public Health

Daniel W. Webster, M.P.H., The Johns Hopkins University School of Hygiene and Public Health

Mark D. Widome, M.D., M.P.H., Pennsylvania State University College of Medicine

Thanks to the National Association for the Education of Young Children, Washington, D.C., for the use of their materials.

Thanks to Subjects & Predicates for source photographs that were used for some of the illustrations in Unit E and Unit F.

Thanks to SCIPP (Statewide Comprehensive Injury Prevention Program), Massachusetts Department of Public Health, for the use of their materials.

Special thanks to selected members of the American Academy of Pediatrics for reviewing and refining the materials.

These manuscripts were reviewed by the National Academy of Sciences Institute of Medicine, Committee to Advise the American National Red Cross.

Funding for this project was provided in part by the U.S. Department of the Army, contract number MDA903-87-C-0736.

Field representatives providing advice and guidance through the American Red Cross Child Care Course Advisory Committee included:
Lin Arnette, Virginia Capital Chapter, Richmond, Va.

Carolyn Branson, R.N., Eastern Operations Headquarters, Alexandria, Va.

William Calhoun, M.A., Field Service Manager, Midwestern Operations Headquarters

Julianne Crevatin, M.P.H., Seattle-King County Chapter, Seattle, Wash.

Carolyn Elliott, Bluegrass Area Chapter, Lexington, Ky.

Angie Turner-Elliott, R.N., Hawkeye Chapter, Waterloo, Iowa

Deborah MacSwain, American Red Cross, Air Force Academy Station, Peterson Air Force Base, Colorado Springs, Colo.

C. Ray McLain, R.N., M.S.N., Assistant Professor, Auburn University at Montgomery, Montgomery, Ala.

Joan Manning, M.P.H., Heartland Chapter, Omaha, Nebr.

Sandra Nation, M.Ed., U.S. Department of the Army Child Development Services, Washington, D.C.

Josephine Otis, R.N., B.S.N., Metropolitan Atlanta Chapter, Atlanta, Ga.

Carol Weis, M.S., Nashville Area Chapter, Nashville, Tenn.

Acknowledgments

Red Cross chapters that participated in field tests included:

East Bay Chapter
Oakland, Calif.

Hawkeye Chapter
Waterloo, Iowa

Metropolitan Atlanta Chapter
Atlanta, Ga.

American Red Cross of Massachusetts Bay
Boston, Mass.

Nashville Area Chapter
Nashville, Tenn.

Seattle-King County Chapter
Seattle, Wash.

American Red Cross, Fort Lewis, Wash.

American Red Cross, Fort Carson, Colo.

American Red Cross, Letterman Army Medical Center, Presidio of San Francisco, Calif.

Contents

About the American Red Cross Child Care Course

The American Red Cross has developed the Child Care Course to improve the quality of child care nationwide by training caregivers in health, safety, and child development. Because more women with children have entered the paid labor force, the population of children requiring child care has expanded rapidly and will continue to expand. This has created a critical shortage of high-quality child care in the United States. The quality is directly affected both by the training and by the relevant experience of the child care staff. Millions of child care workers are employed in the United States, but many of these caregivers have received little or no training. The American Red Cross Child Care Course is being delivered through the Red Cross chapters to train all caregivers, whether they are based in centers or in homes.

The American Red Cross Child Care Course consists of the following 7 units:

Health and Safety Units
A. Preventing Childhood Injuries
B. Infant and Child First Aid
C. Preventing Infectious Diseases
D. Caring for Ill Children

Child Development Units
E. Learning About Child Development
F. Communicating With Children and Parents
G. Recognizing and Reporting Child Abuse

The Child Development Units are included in this workbook. In addition to the 7 units of the Child Care Course, the Red Cross encourages all caregivers to take the American Red Cross CPR: Infant and Child course.

American Red Cross Child Care Course: Learning About Child Development

Contents

About the Learning About Child Development Unit

Most adults who care for young children already know about many of the major ways children develop. For example, they know the ages at which children generally first smile, grow their first teeth, and take their first steps.

Children's lives are filled with many firsts, but you must also know about many of the other, less familiar, happenings of children's development. You need to know that not all children of the same age develop at the same rate, but that most children develop in a predictable and orderly way. You need to know children's common behaviors at various stages of development. And you need to know how to encourage children to grow and develop the best they can at every age and stage of life.

This unit will help you to learn about the ages and stages of child development and the many ways infants, toddlers, and pre-school children change and grow. The unit will also help you know how to allow children to be unique individuals within a group setting.

What You Will Learn

This unit will teach you—
1. Which are the major changes in children's development from infancy to 5 years of age.
2. How to encourage children's growth and development.
3. Which are the general characteristics of most infants, of most toddlers, and of most preschoolers.
4. How to use developmentally appropriate practices to match toys, games, equipment, and teaching strategies with children's different ages and stages.
5. Which are an infant's most important needs and how the caregiver can meet them.
6. How to help a toddler to learn to use the toilet.
7. How to help preschoolers develop language skills.
8. How caregivers play several roles when they care for children.

Further Information

For further information about child development, write the American Academy of Pediatrics, P.O. Box 927, Elk Grove Village, IL 60009-0927.

Activity 1
Orientation

Objective

After you have finished this activity, you will be able to do the following:
1. Tell the unit requirements

Lessons

- Your instructor will discuss the unit with you and what you must do to pass it. The unit requirements are—
  - Satisfactory performance on the test—80 percent or higher (or 20 correct answers).
  - Attendance of the class for the entire unit.
- You will review the contents of the workbook.

Learning About Child Development Unit Agenda

Activity	Topic
1	Orientation
2	Introductions
3	Learning About Development
4	*For Those Who Care* Video, Part 1: "Beginnings/Infants"
5	Infant Development—Getting a Grasp on the World
6	*For Those Who Care* Video, Part 2: "Stepping Out/Toddlers"
7	Toddler Development—Thinking BIG
Break	
8	*For Those Who Care* Video, Part 3: "Ready, Set, Go/Preschoolers"
9	Preschooler Development—Off and Running
10	Test and Unit Evaluation

Activity 2
Introductions

Objectives

After you have finished this activity, you will be able to do the
following:
1. Use the All About You sheet to tell the group about yourself
2. Tell why you are taking this unit

Lesson

- Fill out the All About You sheet. The sheet is on the next page.

All About You

Fill in the blanks.

1. What is your name? _____

2. Where do you work? _____

3. What is your job there?_____

4. How old are the children in your group?_____

5. Why are you taking this unit?_____

6. What do you hope to learn?_____

_____

_____

Activity 3
Learning About Development

Learning Objectives

After you have finished this activity, you will be able to do the following:
1. Identify some of the factors that affect how children develop
2. Name the 4 areas of child development and give examples of each
3. Explain the meaning of *developmentally appropriate*

Lessons

- There are 4 areas of child development. These include *physical* development, *cognitive* development, *emotional* development, and *social* development. Development means the process that children go through as they change, grow, and mature. All children have their own heredity, personality, and experiences that affect how they develop.
- Write the meanings of the terms below as the instructor discusses them. Use Appendix A, The Word List, if you need help.

1. Physical development

the body — body changes

_____

_____

_____

_____

_____

2. Cognitive development

in nursing

change is the child goes thru usien

their minds

_____

_____

_____

3. Emotional development

expressing feelings about themselves &
world around them

_____

_____

_____

_____

These areas overlap

E-7

4. Social development

getting along with others

_____

_____

_____

_____

_____

- Most children grow in an orderly and predictable way in all 4 areas of development. For example, most children crawl before they can walk, and they understand words before they can talk.
- The stages of child development are commonly classified by the following age groups:
  - Infants—From birth to 12 months of age
  - Toddlers—From 1 year to 3 years of age
  - Preschoolers—From 3 years to 5 years of age

  Children's abilities can vary greatly within these stages as well as between them.
- The term *developmentally appropriate* is basic to your understanding of child development. Turn to Appendix A, The Word List, to look up the definition of the term. You can use what you learn about child development and what you know about each child to make developmentally appropriate choices in the child care setting.

  Discipline must also be developmentally appropriate. For toddlers, you should limit rules to a few basic, positive guidelines. But for preschoolers, you should allow the children to help set rules.

  Developmentally appropriate practices are the many ways you use what you know about how children grow and develop to plan ways for children to play and to learn at the same time. You must offer children learning experiences through planned activities that are just right for each child's age.
- When you understand how children develop, you can provide them with appropriate and safe play activities to allow them to grow and to learn. Children learn about their world through play. For further information, turn to Appendix B, The Importance of Play; Appendix C, Growth and Development Charts; and Appendix D, Discipline and Children. You may refer to these appendixes at any time during class.

Activity 4
For Those Who Care Video, Part 1: "Beginnings/Infants"

Lesson

• Watch the video.

Activity 5
Infant Development—Getting a Grasp On the World

Learning Objectives

After you have finished this activity, you will be able to do the following:

1. Tell some basic needs that most infants have
2. Tell some behaviors that most infants have in common
3. Describe the developmentally appropriate practices you can use to encourage infant development
4. Show or tell a game, song, fingerplay, nursery rhyme, or poem appropriate for infants

Lessons

- Most infants have many basic needs in common. You must meet the following needs:
  - Infants need food, shelter, and clothing.
  - Infants need people to trust.
  - Infants need to give and to receive love.
  - Infants need a flexible routine.
  - Infants need comforting surroundings.
  - Infants need consistency.
  - Infants need to be talked to.
  - Infants need to be held and cuddled.

- Infants need to communicate with others.
- Infants need to learn about others.
- Infants need to play.
- Infants need a safe environment for learning and for growing.
- Infants need people to understand their own styles and special needs.
- Infants need to believe their needs will be met.
- Infants need to be touched and held if they are to grow up to be happy and healthy. Talk to infants, hold their hands, and interact with them as much as you can.

- Most infants have many behaviors in common, and most of the things you do for infants affect all 4 areas of development. This means you must respond to and must encourage infants in all 4 areas of development, often at the same time. For example, when an infant smiles at someone, all 4 areas of development are at work—physical development (use of muscles); cognitive development (recognition); emotional development (pleasure); and social development (responsiveness). You should respond to the smiling infant by smiling and speaking warmly. In the list below, when a behavior involves more than one area of development, the additional area or areas of development are included in parentheses.

Common Behaviors

Developmentally Appropriate Practices

Physical

1. Infants cry to have their needs met (also cognitive).

1. You must respond quickly and warmly to an infant's crying and try to figure out why the infant is crying. Infants who are responded to in this way during their early months are less likely to cry as much later in their first year. They learn to trust that their needs will be met.

2. Infants touch, hold, and throw objects.

2. You must provide balls, rattles, mobiles; soft, cuddly, washable toys; and squeaky toys to stimulate infants.

3. Infants roll, sit, crawl, walk, and climb.

3. You must provide safe places for an infant to explore. Infants need objects to hold onto, to pull themselves up on, to reach for, to walk around, and to climb on. To encourage an infant to roll over, you can gently roll the infant from back to stomach or put the infant next to an unbreakable mirror. As infants are able to move around more, you will have to be more and more careful to provide a safe and stimulating environment.

Learning About Child Development

Cognitive

1. Infants make sounds, understand words, and talk.

2. Infants use the 5 senses to hear, to touch, to see, to smell, and to taste.

3. Infants handle objects.

1. You should hold, talk with, and look at the infant. You should imitate the infant's expressions and sounds and should talk to an infant about the world around him or her. You may mimic an infant's expressions or sounds, but when you speak to the infant, pronounce and use words correctly. You should try to speak at least a few words to a child in the child's home language if that language is not English.

2. You should provide appropriate equipment (safe, colorful, and right for the infant's age), a variety of foods (with different colors, tastes, textures, and odors), and appropriate toys (safe, colorful, and too big to fit into an infant's mouth; some toys should make noise).

3. You should provide nesting cups and cubes, pots and pans, wooden beads too large to fit completely into the infant's mouth, blocks, push and pull toys, and other appropriate toys and household items.

Social/Emotional

1. Infants play with others *(also cognitive)*.

2. Infants trust family members and the caregiver.

3. Infants fear separation from the people they love, trust, and have bonded to, and they fear strangers *(also cognitive)*. (This fear starts by 7 months of age and continues until about 18 months of age. It is also known as separation/ stranger anxiety.)

1. You should play games, such as peekaboo, that help develop the infant's concept of object permanence. (*Object permanence* is the understanding that something still exists even though it is out of sight.) You should provide an environment that encourages and stimulates play opportunities. Infants often play alone, but they will also play side by side with each other (parallel play). Older infants may play together briefly, such as when 2 of them pound a drum together (cooperative play). Infants often become friends of each other.

2. You should respond to an infant's needs by being comforting, flexible, and understanding. You may want to have a rocking chair to sit in while holding the infant. You should also let the infant know you can be counted on for consistent and loving care.

3. You should help infants adjust to the child care setting by setting up a homelike environment, including familiar objects, and by reassuring them that the parent will return. All children appreciate honesty. If an infant protests when a parent leaves, don't trick the infant by distracting attention while the parent sneaks away. Greet all children when they arrive and say goodbye when they leave, and encourage parents to do the same. You should help parents feel proud that their infant cares so much about them and that the infant is developing in both the emotional and cognitive areas.

- Your instructor will assign you one or 2 partners. You will teach each other games, songs, fingerplays, poems, or nursery rhymes appropriate for infants. If you need any help, turn to Appendix E, Infants' Play Activities.

  You can use the space below to write the words or directions to any new game, song, fingerplay, poem, or nursery rhyme that you would like to remember.

_____

_____

_____

_____

_____

_____

_____

_____

_____

_____

_____

_____

Activity 6
For Those Who Care Video, Part 2: "Stepping Out/Toddlers"

Lesson

- Watch the video.

Activity 7
Toddler Development—Thinking BIG

Learning Objectives

After you have finished this activity, you will be able to do the following:
1. Name several behaviors that most toddlers have in common
2. Describe developmentally appropriate practices you can use to encourage toddler development
3. Tell what toddlers must be able to do before they are ready to learn how to use the toilet

Lessons

- Most toddlers have some behaviors, traits, and abilities in common. These include the following:
  - Toddlers have improved large-muscle and small-muscle skills.
  - Toddlers are very active.
  - Toddlers learn by using their bodies.

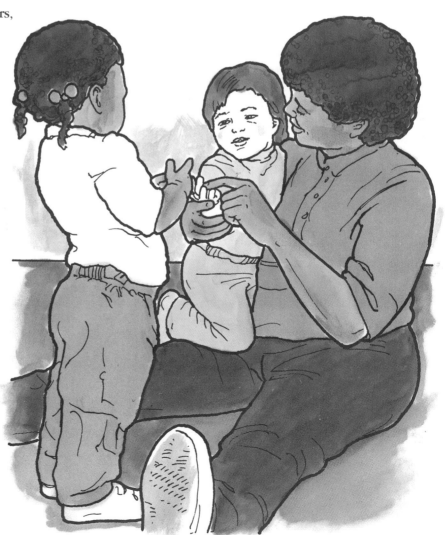

Learning About Child Development

- Toddlers can use language.
- Toddlers have better problem-solving abilities.
- Toddlers understand that objects they can't see still exist.
- Toddlers are determined.
- Toddlers like repetition.
- Toddlers are affectionate.
- Toddlers can sometimes control their own behavior.
- Toddlers like to do things for themselves.
- Toddlers need to succeed.
- Toddlers have very strong imaginations.
- Like infants, toddlers grow and change in predictable and orderly ways, and each toddler is unique. Toddlers like to think of themselves as "big" people, and they seem to be in a hurry to grow up. Toddlers imitate adults, so act the way you want them to act. Most toddlers have several behaviors in common. You must use several developmentally appropriate practices to encourage toddler development. The common behaviors and the developmentally appropriate practices are listed below.

Common Behaviors

Physical

1. Toddlers walk alone, run, and jump (large-muscle skills).

2. Toddlers pour, pound, and stack (small-muscle skills).

3. Toddlers begin toilet training *(also cognitive, social, and emotional)*.

Developmentally Appropriate Practices

1. You should provide toddlers with lots of playthings that develop large-muscle skills, such as blocks, bells, drums, brooms, cranks, child-sized grocery carts and wagons, and riding toys that steer.

2. You should provide toddlers with lots of playthings that develop small-muscle skills, such as sand and water, pounding benches, table toys, one-inch-wide paint brushes, tempera (poster) paints, finger paints, watercolor markers, and large sheets of paper. (You should hang their drawings or paintings low on the wall where everyone can see them.) Turn to Appendix F, Toy Safety, for further information.

3. (Toilet training will be discussed later in this activity.)

Learning About Child Development

Cognitive

1. Toddlers talk.

1. You can encourage language development by—
   - Talking with and listening to toddlers. Answer their questions in ways that make sense to them.
   - Speaking some words in the language the toddler speaks at home if that language is not English.
   - Reading to toddlers and allowing them to discuss the story and pictures.
   - Giving toddlers a chance to talk, ask questions, look at books, and scribble on their own.
   - Taking toddlers on walks and short trips and pointing out details.
   - Talking about interesting features of the world around them so that toddlers learn to notice details.
   - Asking questions that can't be answered with *yes* or *no*.
   - Listening to and then responding to toddlers with complete ideas, rather than with just one or 2 words. (When responding, you may restate what the toddler says in correct words, or you may add more to the toddler's ideas. For example, if the toddler says "Me do" while putting on a jacket, you might say, "You want to zip it yourself.")

2. Toddlers solve problems and understand that objects still exist when they can't be seen.

2. You can encourage refinement of thinking skills by—
   - Encouraging toddlers to recognize and to solve real problems and helping them to make sense of cause and effect. For example, you can point out that if they push a ball, the ball rolls.
   - Playing simple games such as peekaboo and other hide-and-seek games to help toddlers learn that people and things don't go away permanently when they are out of sight. When a child is dressing, you can talk about arms, legs, and heads that temporarily go out of sight and say, "Where is your arm? Here it comes!"

3. Toddlers help take care of their own daily needs.

3. You can encourage the development of self-help skills by doing the following:
   - Allowing toddlers to get dressed, to brush teeth, to eat, and eventually, to go to the toilet without much help.
   - Involving toddlers in everyday activities. Toddlers need to feel a part of the adult world. Some everyday activities for toddlers include—
     - Setting the table.
     - Feeding pets.
     - Folding laundry.
     - Helping prepare simple foods, such as spreading jam.
     - Wiping off the table.
     - Washing hands.

Social/Emotional

1. Toddlers have increased self-esteem and self-discipline.

1. You can help a toddler develop self-esteem and self-discipline by—
   - Giving personal attention and by praising the toddler and what he or she does. A toddler will become an eager learner and friendly person if he or she feels good about himself or herself. Like all children, toddlers should be treated with respect.
   - Letting a toddler have some control over his or her life by letting the toddler take the initiative and make decisions.
   - Acting in ways you expect children to act: generously, warmly, lovingly, and thoughtfully.
   - Setting up a few simple rules for toddlers to follow, and by reminding them to follow the rules.
   - Showing interest in what the toddler is trying to say.

2. Toddlers play with others at times.

3. Toddlers learn to become more independent by refusing to do what they are asked.

2. You can help toddlers learn to share more easily when you give toddlers chances to share by providing 2 or more of the most popular toys, by helping toddlers settle fights on their own, and by setting simple rules of behavior. However, because most toddlers are self-centered, they are not yet ready to share toys.

3. You can encourage toddler independence by allowing toddlers to make choices. You can offer them real choices—for example, whether to play with a tricycle or truck, or to eat an apple or a pear. This helps toddlers to learn to make decisions for themselves and to experience the consequences of their decisions.

• All caregivers have at least one process they will have to deal with—that is, helping a child who is still wearing diapers learn to use the toilet. This is called *toilet training*. Some educators prefer the term *toilet learning*. You can use a simple formula to decide if the time is right to help children learn how to use the toilet. You can use this formula to make decisions about other developmental tasks, too.

First, you must *identify the developmental task*. (The child needs to learn to use the toilet.) Second, you must *list skills needed* to accomplish the task. (The child must be developed enough in all 4 areas to be able to learn to use the toilet.) Third, you must *set goals* that are realistic. (The child uses the toilet at the child care setting.) The list below shows you how the formula works.

  • **Identify the developmental task.** The child is wearing diapers and needs to learn to use the toilet.
  • **List skills needed**.
    (With all the skills needed for toilet training, children are usually not ready to start before age 2.)
    1. The child has the desire to learn how to use the toilet.
    2. The child can sense how his or her body feels when he or she needs to go to the toilet.
    3. The child can control his or her bladder and bowel muscles until time to go to the bathroom.
    4. The child can give himself or herself enough time to get to the bathroom.
    5. The child can talk, so the child can tell the caregiver when he or she needs to use the toilet and can ask for help with opening the door, if needed.
    6. The child can undress and dress himself or herself, or ask for help.
    7. The child can climb up to and sit comfortably on the toilet.
  • **Set the goal**: The child uses the toilet.

- Adults can help make toilet training a success by doing the following:
  - Adults must let the child's development determine when to introduce toilet training.
  - Adults can help children to see toilet training as a new source of pride and independence and as a sign of being grown up.
  - Adults can talk about how good it feels to be dry.
  - Adults can provide child-size toilets or adapter seats and stools for adult-size toilets.
  - Adults can ask the child to help clean up any messes without making a big fuss about them—accidents happen.
  - Adults should not offer bribes or rewards, such as candy or toys, for going to the toilet successfully. The caregiver can help the child be proud of his or her own accomplishment with a smile and a few words such as, "Doesn't it feel good to be so grown up?"
  - Adults can observe children at play and can learn to recognize when to remind a child about using the toilet. A child may be so busy that he or she may forget to use the toilet.
  - Caregivers and parents should work closely together. For example, the caregiver can ask parents to dress the child in clothes that are easy to take down and to put back on, such as clothes without zippers or snaps.
  - Caregivers and parents should decide together when a child is ready for toilet training. Good ongoing communication between the home and the child care setting is important during the toilet training process.
  - Adults should be aware that new situations, such as a new infant at home or moving, may upset the child temporarily and may cause the child to lose interest in learning how to use the toilet.

Note: Potty chairs are not recommended for the child care setting because of the sanitation requirements and the chance of spreading disease from child to child. Potty chairs may be all right for home use.

Activity 8
For Those Who Care Video, Part 3: "Ready, Set, Go/ Preschoolers"

Lesson

• Watch the video.

Activity 9
Preschooler Development—
Off and Running

Learning Objectives

After you have finished this activity, you will be able to do the following:
1. List several activities and play experiences that encourage preschooler development
2. Describe developmentally appropriate practices you can use to encourage preschooler development
3. Tell how you can encourage the development of preschooler language skills
4. Tell why making dough clay is a developmentally appropriate activity for preschoolers

Lesson

• Preschoolers need many activities and play experiences to help them develop in all 4 areas. Remember what you saw in the video. The activities include the following:
  • Sharing
  • Talking

- Listening to someone
- Looking at books
- Painting
- Building with blocks
- Pretending and role-playing
- Dictating a letter
- Blowing bubbles
- Jumping
- Running
- Climbing
- Playing with sand
- Hammering
- Cooking
- Singing, clapping, and dancing or moving to music
- Doing water play
- Playing with puzzles
- Most preschoolers have some behaviors in common. You can use developmentally appropriate practices to encourage preschooler development. The behaviors and developmentally appropriate practices are listed below.

Common Behaviors

Physical

1. Preschoolers like to run, climb, and ride bikes. Preschoolers become better at combining several skills, such as kicking a ball and riding a tricycle, to develop large muscles.

2. Preschoolers become better at combining several skills, such as building with small blocks, drawing, and cutting with scissors, to develop small muscles.

3. Preschoolers want to do self-help activities such as dressing, toileting, and eating.

Developmentally Appropriate Practices

1. You should provide toys for active play and should provide safe playground equipment.

2. You should provide activities to encourage the development of small-muscle skills, including—
   - Cooking, dress up, and pretend play.
   - Building with blocks.
   - Painting.
   - Writing and drawing.
   - Hammering.
   - Doing puzzles.
   - Shelling a hard-boiled egg.
   - Turning pages in a picture book.
   - Pasting together small bits of paper.
   - Picking up pebbles.
   - Snapping small interlocking blocks together.

3. You should allow time for preschoolers to do things for themselves. For example, give preschoolers time to fasten buttons and zippers.

Cognitive

1. Preschoolers expand their language skills by reading, drawing, and speaking.

1. You can encourage language skills by—
   - Having lots of picture books on hand for preschoolers to look at and to talk about.
   - Pointing out signs during a walk and telling what the signs mean.
   - Showing preschoolers how adults use notes and lists to keep track of things.
   - Helping older preschoolers who want to try to write their names or make signs for certain activities.
   - Showing older preschoolers how to hold a crayon, a marker, or a pencil or pen.
   - Helping older preschoolers to recognize and write letters or words correctly.
   - Writing down the stories preschoolers make up.
   - Leaving space for preschoolers to draw pictures to go with their stories.
   - Letting preschoolers spell words in their own way.
   - Asking preschoolers to retell a story or to tell about their own pictures.

2. Preschoolers ask questions.

2. You can encourage the preschooler to be curious by allowing the child to ask many *how* and *why* questions about the ways things work and letting the preschooler find his or her own answer. (Organizing a week around a theme, such as springtime, baby animals, or safety, can help children learn about new things.) You can also allow the child to take objects apart and put them back together again or to fix objects that are broken.

    You should encourage creativity and imagination. For example, you can provide time for pretend play and allow the preschooler to act out what it feels like to be someone else. The difference between reality and fantasy is not always clear for preschoolers. You can help them figure out what can really happen and what is pretend by asking open-ended questions that get children to think about their own experiences.

3. Preschoolers can follow simple directions, solve some problems, and make many decisions.

3. You can encourage the preschooler to follow directions by giving the child activities that require following a sequence of steps, such as following a recipe or feeding a pet. You should also allow the preschooler to do things that involve solving problems and making decisions. The child might sort things into 2 categories, such as colors (red objects in one pile, blue objects in another), or into overlapping categories, such as "round and red" or "square and blue."

Learning About Child Development

Social/Emotional

1. Preschoolers develop self-esteem.

2. Preschoolers develop self-discipline.

3. Preschoolers can make more complicated decisions.

1. You can help the preschooler feel good about himself or herself by encouraging the child to feel confident, by treating the child with respect, and by showing interest in what the child has to say. A confident child has more self-esteem and is more likely to try new things, to learn more about the world, and to lead a productive life.

2. You should practice and model self-discipline because the preschooler will behave the way an adult does. You must control your emotions and behavior. For example, if you are angry, use words, not actions, to express and resolve your anger.

3. You should allow the preschooler to make more difficult choices and decisions. A play activity children choose for themselves can interest them for half an hour or more. They'll invent their own problems to solve.

- You are going to put into practice all you have learned about how to encourage child development through play. You are going to join a small group to make dough clay. One person in your group will act as the caregiver. The others will act as the children. The recipe for dough clay appears on the flip chart and also in Appendix G, Dough Clay Recipe. When you are through making dough clay, the instructor will ask you to answer the following questions:
  - How does making dough clay contribute to children's physical, cognitive, emotional, and social development?
  - Were the "children" happy about how much they participated in the group activity?
  - How did each group decide to measure, pour, stir, and add color to the dough clay? How did the "children" feel about the way these decisions were made? Did they get to make any decisions?
  - How did the "caregiver" feel about involving the "children" in the dough clay making? Did the "children" feel that they got to do enough?

- Caregivers must be many things to many children of many different ages. Working with children is a big challenge and when you learn to work with them successfully, you will feel proud of yourself and what you can do. Some of the roles you play include the following:
  - You use developmentally appropriate practices to encourage development in all 4 areas.
  - You provide safe situations in which children can use their bodies to test physical limits and to practice new skills.
  - You offer a wide range of books, toys, games, objects from many cultures, everyday items, and other equipment so children can select those that are most appealing and best suited to their own abilities.
  - You encourage children to learn through play, whether the children are playing alone, in pairs, or in small groups.
  - You set up play areas so that children can see the materials they have to choose from and can easily return them.
  - You help children find words to use to interact with each other so that they don't have to use their fists, feet, or teeth. (Don't wait until children are angry or upset to help them learn to use words to express their feelings.)
  - You ask questions, provide help, and are available.
  - You help children to feel good about themselves by encouraging them, by reinforcing positive behaviors, and by providing opportunities for success.
  - You allow each child to be a unique individual within a group setting.
- For further information, turn to Appendix H, Caregivers Helping Children.

Activity 10
Test and Unit Evaluation

Objective

After you have finished this activity, you will be able to do the following:

1. Complete the test

Lessons

- The test that the instructor will give you has 25 questions about what you learned in this class. Answer the questions on the answer sheet. You must score 80 percent or higher (or answer 20 or more questions correctly) to pass this unit.

- Your instructor will also give you a unit evaluation sheet. Please tell us what you thought of this unit by filling out this sheet and returning it to the instructor.

- Thank you for your participation in the American Red Cross Child Care Course. By taking all of the units of the Child Care Course, you are showing your commitment to giving the best possible child care. Now that you understand the information and skills presented, you will be able to put your caring and concern for children into action.

Appendixes

The Word List

Behavior—The way a person responds to other people or to the surroundings.

Cognitive development—Learning, or the changes and growth in thinking that take place inside children's minds. As children learn from experiences, their behavior and thinking change.

Culture—Shared customs, language, child-rearing practices, religious beliefs, or other similarities among people who are from the same area, country, or ethnic group.

Development—The process that children go through as they change, grow, and mature. The 4 areas in which children develop are the physical, cognitive, emotional, and social areas.

Developmentally appropriate—A term used to describe activities and surroundings that are chosen because they are right for children of a certain age and also take into account each child's individual needs.

Discipline—Guidance and teaching techniques that promote good behavior, discourage bad behavior, and promote self-esteem and self-control.

Emotional development—The way children's feelings about themselves and their world change and mature.

Eye-hand coordination—Ability to coordinate vision with the movement of fingers, hands, and arms.

Growth—The process of increasing or expanding in size.

Heredity—Characteristics that children inherit from their parents.

Infants—Children from birth to 12 months of age.

Limits—Reasonable rules to protect children and to help them control their own behavior.

Motor skills—Skills involving motion or the ability to move. Large-muscle skills are used for moving the major muscles, such as those in the arms and legs. Small-muscle skills are used for moving the smaller muscles, such as those in the fingers.

Object permanence—The understanding that something still exists even though it is out of sight.

Open-ended questions—Questions that can be answered correctly in many ways, not only with a single answer.

Physical development—Body changes that children experience as they grow and mature.

Preschoolers—Children from 3 years to 5 years of age.

Pretend play—Make-believe or fantasy activities that help children try out different roles and behaviors.

Self-concept—The way a person thinks and feels about himself or herself.

Self-discipline—A person's ability to control his or her own behavior.

Separation/Stranger anxiety—An infant's fear of separation from the people he or she loves, trusts, and has bonded to, and an infant's fear of strangers. The fear begins by 7 months of age and continues until about 18 months of age.

Social development—The way a child learns how to get along with others.

Toddlers—Children from one year to 3 years of age.

The Importance of Play

Play helps children to learn about their world and helps them grow in all 4 areas of development. Children learn through play, whether the play is self-directed or consists of developmentally appropriate activities provided by the caregiver.

Physical

- Play enables a child's small- and large-muscle coordination to develop.
- Play enhances eye-hand coordination and muscle development.

Physical activities include running, jumping, climbing, lifting, pulling, pedaling, reaching, hopping, dancing, skipping, rolling, bending, stacking blocks, shaking bells, doing puzzles, pouring, drawing, pasting, and swinging.

Cognitive

- Play fosters a child's language, reading, and writing development.
- Play stimulates a child's imagination.
- Play helps a child learn the difference between fantasy and reality.
- Play expands a child's curiosity, creative thinking, and skills.
- Play enables a child to explore cause and effect.
- Play provides new information about the world.
- Play gives a child the chance to organize information.
- Play allows a child to figure out how to solve problems.
- Play enables a child to try out new roles.
- Play sets the stage for a child to learn how to think through ideas and problems.

Cognitive activities include figuring out how to make a block structure, deciding which items to paste on a collage, selecting colors for a painting, making a grocery list, seeing "what happens when . . . ," working out the rules to a game, looking in a mirror, playing with dolls or toy animals, and talking on the telephone.

Emotional

- Play enables a child to feel good about himself or herself.
- Play allows a child to express emotions and try out possible solutions to problems.
- Play supports a child's willingness to persist at a task.
- Play helps a child develop self-control.

Emotional development is enhanced by play experiences that include being able to complete a task independently, having an adult acknowledge the child's success, feeling free to express feelings safely but honestly (such as shouting rather than hitting when angry), and being given opportunities to take more responsibility for self.

Social

- Play gives children opportunities to learn to do things together.
- Play sets the stage for social problem solving, sharing, and resolving disagreements by talking.
- Play helps a child develop respect for others.
- Play helps a child to learn to see things from another person's point of view.

Social development is enhanced by play experiences that include opportunities to share, play together, and work out problems without adult interference, thinking about "how it would feel if . . . ." Children can learn through play to consider whether an action is fair to others. When children play with caregivers, they should have a chance to observe positive behaviors such as kindness, sharing, and fairness.

Growth and Development Charts

Growth and Development Chart

Infants—Birth to 12 Months

Common Behaviors
Physical
Cries when hungry or uncomfortable.

Smiles.

Pushes up from chest.

Holds up and turns head.

Sucks on hand and other objects.

Keeps hands closed or partly closed much of the time.

Likes to touch, grasp, and hold objects.

Rolls over by about 4 months, sits up by about 7 months, and crawls.

Teeth start to come in by about 6 months.

Drops, throws, and bangs on objects.

Begins to pull up to stand; bounces, climbs, and takes steps.

Begins to drink from cup as well as breast and bottle.

Cognitive
Uses senses—hearing, touching, seeing, smelling, tasting—to learn.

Enjoys looking at slowly moving, brightly colored objects.

Babbles, makes sounds, imitates sounds.

Is fascinated by small objects.

Handles objects from hand to hand.

Likes music, has favorite tunes and sounds.

Makes sounds that sound like words, such as "ma-ma" and "da-da."

Understands more than he or she can say.

Looks for dropped objects or hidden faces.

Stacks 2 cubes.

Imitates adult facial expressions.

Social/Emotional
Needs comfort, love, security.

Smiles, especially at faces.

Enjoys being with people.

Plays with people.

Shows needs, anger, and frustration by crying and kicking.

Develops fear of strangers.

Gets upset when someone leaves the room.

Trusts family members and caregivers.

What Caregiver Should Do
Smile at the infant.

Talk to and sing to the infant in the home language, if possible.

Move infants often to new body positions or places in the room.

Hold and cuddle the infant.

Provide toys and simple games that encourage movement and thinking.

Avoid overstimulation before bedtime or naptime.

Watch for signs of discomfort and fatigue.

Follow parents' instructions for feeding.

Change diapers regularly.

Report bowel movements to parents.

Always say goodbye and manage parents' goodbyes.

Toys and Games
Mobiles of different patterns and bright colors

Pat-a-cake, peekaboo, bye-bye

Squeaky toys, rattles

Stuffed animals, soft dolls with no removable parts

Nesting cups, blocks

Balls to roll

Pots and pans, wooden spoons

Large wooden beads or spools (too big to fit entirely into the infant's mouth) strung on a knotted and tightly strung cord

Large or medium-sized blocks

Bells to shake

Unbreakable mirrors

Sturdy picture books with thick cardboard pages

Push toys

Safety During Play
Remove any small articles left on the floor, such as pins, beans, peanuts, and coins.

Remove toys or objects that have broken pieces or sharp edges.

Remove all safety pins. (If they must be used, close them securely.)

Never leave the child unprotected on a bed or changing table or unsupervised in a carriage, highchair, stroller, or playpen.

Cover electrical outlets.

Avoid using tablecloths that hang over edges of the table.

Avoid a clutter of small things on the floor.

Remove jewelry, if necessary, when holding the baby.

Lock safety gates.

Keep shoelaces tied.

Be sure that no lead paint is in the child care setting.

Lock up all medicines, poisons, cleaning solutions, knives, and other dangerous items.

Keep plastic bags and cords away from children.

Growth and Development Chart

Toddlers 1 to 3 Years

Common Behaviors
Physical
Walks alone, runs, and jumps.
Opens boxes, pulls toys behind him or her.
Pours, pounds, and stacks.
Has 6 to 16 temporary teeth.
Chews solid food.
Begins to use the toilet.

Cognitive
Likes to play; begins to do things on his or her own.
Pokes fingers in holes; turns knobs and dials.
Reacts to familiar comments; starts to talk.
Enjoys building activities.
Understands that out of sight doesn't mean something no longer exists.
Chooses and hugs favorite toys.
Begins to do self-help routines (feeding, drinking, dressing, etc.)
Explores how things work.
Does the same actions over and over.
Points to objects named by adults.
Uses one hand more than the other.
Follows simple instructions.

Social/Emotional
Begins to develop self-discipline.
Needs attention, love, and security.
Likes to play alone and sometimes alongside others (such as coloring own picture while other children color theirs).
May have temper tantrums when needs are not met.
Has favorite habits or customs.
Is usually friendly.
May refuse to do what he or she is asked.
Begins to be able to share.
Becomes more independent.

What Caregiver Should Do
Be consistent and caring. Show that you like and want to be with the child.
Help the child help himself or herself brush teeth, put on shoes, dress, etc.
Keep up the child's regular habits before sleep time.
Supply appropriate toys.
Play with the child.
Talk with the child to help the child learn more words.
Use short sentences.
Encourage the child to use language to meet his or her needs and express feelings.
Read, sing, or tell stories, songs, and poems.
Use child-sized furniture.
Follow parents' instructions for meals.
Be firm: Set reasonable limits for playtime, mealtime, and sleep time.
Plan rest periods and naps.
Help the child to learn about hazards and to avoid injuries.

Toys and Games
Have lots of popular toys so children don't have to wait to use them.
Action toys: trains, telephones, cars, push-and-pull toys
Large beads to string together
Building blocks; toy people, animals, buildings, cars, and buses
Finger painting, watercolor markers, large blank sheets of paper, crayons and coloring books, other art materials
Sand and water play, mud pies, and clay
Plastic dishes and kitchen tools
Simple musical instruments, record player, action songs
Story books
Puppets, large balls, and cardboard boxes
Puzzles, shapes

Safety During Play
Close safety gates inside and fence gates outside.
Cover electrical outlets.
Supervise children at all times outdoors, in bath tubs, with climbing activities, etc.
Lock up all cleaners, medicines, poisons, and matches.
Keep children away from fireplaces and swimming pools.
Remove breakable objects from the play area.
Remove any toys that have sharp edges, points, or pieces that the child may swallow.
Check on children when they are being unusually quiet.
Mark sliding glass doors with large stickers at children's eye level.
Keep children away from strange animals.
Keep children's shoelaces tied.
Keep plastic bags away from children.

Growth and Development Chart

Preschoolers—3 to 5 Years

Common Behaviors

Physical
Wants to control bodily functions.

Does some self-help routines: dressing, toileting, washing hands, etc.

Walks on tiptoe, runs well forward and backward, and climbs.

Pedals tricycle well.

Combines skills: kicks a ball, builds with small blocks.

Begins to gain control over small muscles used to write and draw.

Cognitive
Knows many words, names of people and things.

Enjoys learning number ideas.

Asks many questions about the world.

Can sort objects, follow directions, sequence activities.

Has a very strong imagination.

Social/Emotional
Has a strong sense of self.

Believes the world turns around him or her.

Enjoys socializing with others.

Needs support in controlling emotions.

Needs comfort, love, security.

Looks up to adults.

Plays cooperatively most of the time (such as coloring the same picture with another child).

May be rowdy.

Learns to see other viewpoints.

Is better able to share and take turns.

Makes more complicated decisions.

Likes regularity and some routine.

What Caregiver Should Do
Let children do as much as possible for themselves.

Tell stories.

Encourage the child to talk.

Let the child pick out toys. Play with the child.

Help the child solve arguments with friends or siblings.

Be firm: set reasonable limits at playtime, mealtime, and sleep time.

Plan plenty of time for self-care routines before meals and sleep time.

Plan active and quiet play with rest periods and naps.

Talk, sing, and read together.

Provide a safe environment and demonstrate safe behavior.

Set up the room to help children put toys away.

Model use of table manners.

Occasionally watch children's programs on TV with the children and talk about the programs.

Talk about the world—what things are made of and how things work.

Toys and Games
Picture puzzles with large pieces

Hide and seek

Follow the leader

Simple board games

Guessing games

Story books

Finger paints, tempera, large sheets of blank paper, other art materials

Songs and recordings

Toys for active play: wagons, balls, and tricycles

Materials they can handle: clay for molding, real musical instruments, tools

Pictures and scraps for cutting and pasting

Dolls and other props for pretend play

Real cooking or carpentry tools

Playground equipment: slides, swings, etc.

Walks outdoors

Safety During Play
Lock up all cleaners, medicines, poisons, and matches.

Supervise play indoors and outdoors.

Keep children away from swimming pools, fireplaces, etc.

Hold children's hands when crossing the street and teach how to cross safely.

Avoid open wires on electric toys and heaters.

Use tricycles and riding toys only on sidewalks or blocked-off areas.

Play ball games away from the street.

Keep sharp objects, sticks, guns, toy caps, arrows, or darts out of children's reach.

Discipline and Children

Discipline is the use of guidance and teaching techniques that promote acceptable behavior and discourage unacceptable behavior. You can help young children develop self-discipline.

Discipline for infants

- Respond as soon as possible when infants cry or kick. They are letting adults know they need something. Your response also helps them learn to trust.
- Always practice self-discipline when caring for children.
- Be warm, calm, and friendly; infants will copy simple adult gestures and expressions.
- Use words to tell the infant what you think he or she is thinking or feeling. The infant needs to learn how to communicate and to express feelings.
- Allow infants to experience the results of their actions on people when it is safe to do. This teaches infants that they have an effect on others.
- Show loving care in all you do. This teaches infants to care about others.
- Respect and understand infant characteristics, such as separation anxiety. Respond appropriately in support of infants as they grow and learn.
- Control your reactions. If you are stressed by upsetting behaviors and if there is enough supervision, leave the room until you are in control of your behavior and feelings.

Discipline for toddlers

- Be generous with toddlers. This helps toddlers to learn not to hoard and to see the value of sharing.
- Continue to use words to express feelings and to help a toddler work out solutions to problems with others. Toddlers will start to use words in similar ways.
- Let toddlers choose between 2 or 3 things. Toddlers need to feel they have some say about what happens to them.
- Allow toddlers to do tasks themselves, when possible. This makes toddlers feel independent, valuable, and strong.
- Limit rules to a few basic, positive guidelines about what toddlers are expected to do.
- Know how toddlers behave. For example, toddlers are not likely to share very often. Toddlers do not wait patiently, so they should not be in situations that require waiting. Toddlers like to say *no* a lot.
- Respect toddlers' feelings. Toddlers will begin to pay attention to the feelings of others, too.

Discipline for preschoolers

- Give preschoolers a chance to decide what happens to them. They are learning to make choices and to resolve problems with others.
- Allow preschoolers to experience the logical and natural results of their own decisions whenever it is safe. This helps them to be responsible people.
- Continue to build the preschoolers' sense of personal worth. Preschoolers are learning to stand up for their own rights.
- Allow preschoolers to talk through their disagreements and solve them for themselves.
- Answer preschoolers' questions—they are eager and curious learners.
- Avoid making or giving bribes, threats, punishments, or excessive rewards for behaviors. These destroy children's self-motivation, rob children of experiencing real consequences, and take away from the good feelings children naturally have when they are friendly and cooperative.
- Allow preschoolers to help set rules. And set a good example by following rules yourself.

Infants' Play Activities

These are examples of activities to share with infants.

Riding Horsies

Sit on a chair or sofa. Hold a very young infant in your lap facing you. Hold the infant's hands, and sing "Trot, Trot, Trot" or recite "Ride a Cock Horse" or some other song or rhyme about horses as you gently bounce the child on your lap. For older infants with more body control, cross one leg over the other and let the infant ride on your ankle, bouncing up and down.

> *Trot, trot, trot,*
> *Trot, trot, trot,*
> *Go and never stop.*
> *Never shall I cease to ride her*
> *'Till I further yet have tried her.*
> *Go and never stop.*
> *Trot, trot, trot, trot, trot*

Peekaboo

When the baby is in a playful mood, loosely cover baby's face with a soft cloth diaper or blanket. Ask "Where's Kim?" Then gently pull the cover off, and with surprise say, "There's Kim!"

Variations include covering your face, covering a favorite toy, and putting the cover between child and a mirror. You can also elaborate on what you say—"Where's Alex? Is he under the sofa? No, he's not there. Is he behind the big chair? No, I don't see him. Where could he be?"

Lullabies

Singing will frequently calm children. Try singing a lullaby—make up your own tune. Use the child's home language whenever possible. Ask parents to translate your favorites and to share their favorites with you.

Nursery rhymes

Recite favorite nursery rhymes. Demonstrate the action, use toy figures, or show pictures of the people, animals, or items mentioned whenever possible. Select rhymes that do not stereotype people by race, sex, age, or other characteristics.

> **Hey, Diddle, Diddle**
> *Hey, Diddle, Diddle!*
> *The cat and the fiddle.*
> *The cow jumped over the moon.*
> *The little dog laughed to see such sport.*
> *And the dish ran away with the spoon.*

> **Hickory, Dickory, Dock**
> *Hickory, Dickory, Dock!*
> *The mouse ran up the clock!*
> *The clock struck one,*
> *And down he run!*
> *Hickory, Dickory, Dock!*

Play together

Play games such as *This Little Piggy* with baby's toes.

This Little Piggy went to market. (hold and wiggle baby's big toe)

This Little Piggy stayed home. (hold and wiggle second toe)

This Little Piggy had roast beef. (hold and wiggle third toe)

This Little Piggy had none. (hold and wiggle fourth toe)

This Little Piggy went "wee-wee-wee" all the way home! (hold and wiggle little toe)

Fun times together

Play "Where's baby's nose?" or "These are baby's ears." Play with each body part on the baby as you name it. Point to your own body parts. Play this game in front of the mirror.

Or walk your fingers up the baby from toe to head, counting 10-9-8-7-6-5-4-3-2-1. Or name the body parts as your fingers walk.

Play "How big's the baby." Show how big the baby is by spreading your arms and saying, "The baby's *this* big!"

Play "Gonna Getcha." Say "I'm gonna getcha!" and surprise the baby with a gentle tickle.

As you read a book or recite a poem about animals, make the sounds the animals make. Be creative!

Some other songs with fingerplays are *Itsy Bitsy Spider; Five Monkeys; Head, Shoulders, Knees, and Toes;* and *The Wheels on the Bus.*

Toy Safety

Toys should be fun and also should help children learn. But some toys can harm children, such as toys that are poorly designed, toys that are not age-appropriate, toys that are used incorrectly, or toys that are broken or worn out. Follow these rules to keep children playing safely and happily:

1. **Give children age-appropriate toys.** For example, if a toy is labeled "for children ages 3 and older," never give it to a child under age 3. It could have small parts or sharp pieces that are dangerous to younger children.

2. **Children who ride bicycles or who are passengers on a bicycle should wear helmets.**

3. **Keep any toy with small parts** (parts that can fit completely into the mouth) **away from children** under age 3 and away from older children who still put toys in their mouths. Children might choke on such toys.

4. **Keep toys made with glass or breakable plastic away from children.**

5. **Deflated or broken balloons are dangerous.** They can suffocate children. Keep balloons away from young children.

6. **If a child uses a riding toy, keep him or her away from stairs, porches, cars, and pools.**

7. **Make sure toy chests have air holes and a lid support or have no lid.** A lid that slams shut could cause head injuries or suffocation.

8. **Check children's toys for the following hazards:**
   - Sharp points, jagged edges, and rough surfaces
   - Small, detachable parts that can be swallowed or stuck in the throat, nose, or ears
   - Cords or strings longer than 12 inches on pull toys
   - Nuts, bolts, and clamps that are loose
   - Very loud noises that can damage hearing
   - Parts that can fly off and harm eyes or hurt others
   - Battery toys with frayed or loose wires. Any electrical wiring should be labeled "UL approved"

Dough Clay Recipe

Soft Dough Clay
(4 or 5 portions)

½ cup plain or iodized salt

4 cups all-purpose flour

1 teaspoon alum (found in spice section of supermarket)

1 cup water

½ cup vegetable oil

food coloring

Mix dry ingredients in plastic bowl. Add oil and water gradually. Knead in food coloring. Clay will not harden or sour. (*Note:* Kneading in food coloring will produce mottled dough clay. For a uniform appearance, mix the food coloring with the water before combining oil and water with dry ingredients.)

(Adapted from *Art: Basic for Young Children,* National Association for the Education of Young Children, 1980.)

Caregivers Helping Children

Every day, the caregiver can take positive steps to help children develop and grow. The following suggestions will help you meet that goal.

- Point out the positive things children do.
- Play more games with children, fitting the rules to the children's abilities.
- Plan activities for children on the basis of what you have learned by watching them play.
- Watch how children behave in order to keep track of how much children grow and learn in all 4 areas of development.
- Make the program's rules tell the children what they can do, not what they cannot do.
- Listen to children talking with each other to find out what interests them, then include those interests in new activities.
- Move mirrors, children's family pictures, children's drawings, and other interesting decorations down to the children's level.
- Put away any toys that do not interest the children. After they have been out of sight for a while, children may find them interesting again.
- Read magazines, pamphlets, or books that will help you learn more about child development.
- Join a local professional caregivers' group to learn about providing better child care.
- Check a variety of children's picture books out of the library; let the children select which they would like.
- If the child comes from another culture, talk with the parents about ways you can help the child become more familiar with that heritage.
- Have children play outdoors as much as possible.

- Ask parents for ideas for activities, field trips, games, songs, and foods for the children.
- Allow ample time for children to play with big blocks, to have fun with sand and water play, to dress up for make-believe play, to do cooking or building projects, etc. Play with the children, too, with songs, fingerplays, or other fun activities to do together on the floor.
- Let the children spend most of their day playing at activities that they choose.
- Put toys out on open shelves within easy reach of the children; have the children return the toys when they are finished playing with them.
- Meet with other caregivers from the Red Cross Child Care Course: Learning About Child Development class to talk about becoming more skilled in your work with children.

American Red Cross Child Care Course: Communicating With Children and Parents

Contents

About the Communicating With Children and Parents Unit

The early childhood years between infancy and the age of 6 are important ones for the child's physical, intellectual, emotional, and social growth and development. During these formative years, the child should be developing self-discipline and self-confidence. The ways in which you and the parent discipline and communicate with the child help shape the child's personality and behavior. When both you and the parent encourage the development of a child's self-discipline, you help the child develop into a cooperative and self-reliant adult.

This unit will teach you many positive ways you can talk to and work with young children so they develop in the best way possible. You will also learn positive ways you can talk to and work with parents. This way, you can help give the child consistent, loving care.

What You Will Learn

This unit will teach you—
1. How discipline and punishment differ.
2. How to achieve effective discipline by setting up an orderly child care setting and an organized program of activities.
3. How adults can practice self-discipline and encourage its development in children.
4. How to guide and to teach children in ways that promote good behavior.
5. How to intervene in a useful way when a child misbehaves.
6. Why children should share in making rules and solving problems.
7. How to use words, gestures, and tone of voice for positive communication with children and parents.

Further Information

For further information about communicating with children and parents, write the American Academy of Pediatrics, P.O. 927, Elk Grove Village, IL 60009-0927; and the National Association for the Education of Young Children, 1834 Connecticut Ave., NW, Washington, DC 20009.

Activity 1
Orientation

Objectives

After you have finished this activity, you will be able to do the following:

1. Tell the unit requirements

Lesson

- Your instructor will discuss the unit with you and what you must do to pass it. The unit requirements are—
  - Satisfactory performance on the test—80 percent or higher (or 20 correct answers).
  - Attendance of the class for the entire unit.
- You will review the contents of the workbook.

Communicating With Children and Parents Unit Agenda

Activity	Topic
1	Orientation
2	Introductions
3	*Appropriate Guidance* Video
4	Communicating With Children
5	Learning About Discipline
Break	
6	Management Plans: Child Behavior
7	Communicating With Parents
8	Test and Unit Evaluation

Activity 2
Introductions

Objectives

After you have finished this activity, you will be able to do the following:

1. Use the All About You sheet to tell the group about yourself
2. Tell why you are taking this unit

Lesson

● Fill out the All About You sheet. The sheet is on the next page.

All About You

Fill in the blanks.

1. What is your name? _____

2. Where do you work? _____

3. What is your job there? _____

4. How old are the children in your group? _____

5. Why are you taking this unit? _____

6. What do you hope to learn? _____

_____

_____

Activity 3
Appropriate Guidance Video

Lesson

- Watch the video.

Activity 4
Communicating With Children

Learning Objectives

After you have finished this activity, you will be able to do the following:
1. Tell how to use words, gestures, and tone of voice for positive communication with children
2. Tell which words are good and bad for use with children
3. List several ways to communicate effectively with children

Lessons

- You must always speak to a child with respect, kindness, and courtesy. You also communicate with children with your body movements and your tone of voice. You can often teach children more by what you do than by what you say.
- Read the Rules for Positive Communication below. These rules will help teach you the right way to communicate with children.

Rules for Positive Communication

1. Always use positive words to direct a child's behavior.
2. Choose words carefully—words affect how a child feels about himself or herself.
3. Model courtesy and respect when you speak to children.
4. Use positive body language and tone of voice, also known as nonverbal communication. Touch children and use eye contact. These are good ways to communicate with and to teach children.
5. Never hurt a child with your words or your actions.
6. Let children know when they are doing something right.
7. Let children know that their needs will be met.

- Your instructor will ask you to discuss one of the topics below with a partner. You and your partner should decide on good ways you could speak to or communicate with children to encourage them to interact with each other, to help children learn a positive behavior, and to encourage self-discipline.

   1. Three toddlers are playing with large interlocking blocks on a coffee table and not in the proper play area.
   2. In 15 minutes, the mother of 4-year-old Gina will pick her up for a doctor's appointment. Gina is afraid to go to the doctor's office.
   3. Ling and Tina, both aged 2, keep pushing the baby carriages they are playing with in front of the doorway, making it hard for the older children to get to the bathroom.
   4. Two-year-old Ellen stands at the top of the slide and refuses to come down. Two other children wait in line behind her.
   5. Five-year-old Arch is helping fold laundry. His stack of folded clothes is about to topple over.
   6. Robert and Sandy decide to clean up the table on which the children have been finger painting—but they are making a terrible mess.
   7. Two infants, Carla and Anthony, wake up from their nap crying. Both need to have their diaper changed, but you decide to diaper Anthony first because he has had a rash lately.

- You will work with a small group to discuss a scenario that the instructor will assign to you. Read the scenarios under the Examples of Positive Communication. Each scenario has both a negative response and a positive response from the video. Write in your own positive response. Remember what you saw in the video.

Examples of Positive Communication

Scenario 1

Katherine and Katie sit together at a table drawing pictures on their own sheets of paper. Katherine starts scribbling on Katie's paper.

Negative response
Katherine, don't mess up Katie's paper. Keep your hands to yourself.

Positive response from the video
Katherine, you have to keep your marks on your own paper. This is yours; it has your name on it. Katie, I am sorry that happened. Here is another for you if you would like to start again.

Another positive response

_____

_____

Scenario 2

Cam and Judy are playing with blocks. Suddenly Cam knocks over the block castle Judy has built.

Negative response
Cam, shame on you for being so mean. Go sit in the corner.

Positive response from the video
Cam, remember, you are only allowed to knock down things _you_ have built. Please leave the block area until you can remember that rule. You can try again later.

Another positive response

_____

_____

Scenario 3

Mary Brice and Ellie are arguing over the use of a magnifier.

Negative response
Girls, girls. Don't be so selfish. Don't you know how to share?

Positive response from the video
Girls, I have something here that will make things look big, too. Mary Brice, you use this magnifier now, and Ellie, you use this one. You can trade in a few minutes.

Another positive response

_____

_____

Scenario 4

Serena says that Bea called her a "dumb-dumb."

Negative response
Serena, anyone who calls another person a "dumb-dumb" is the stupid one. Why don't you slap her?

Positive response from the video
I am sorry. You can tell Bea your name is Serena.

Another positive response

_____

_____

Examples of Positive Communication

Scenario 5

Annie says that Ryan bit her.

Negative response
Ryan, I am going to tell your mother on you so she can spank you at home.

Positive response from the video
I'm sorry Annie, I know that hurts. Ryan, I can't let you hurt other people. Biting hurts. I am very angry.

Another positive response

_____

_____

Scenario 6

Jason wants to continue playing with a puzzle and doesn't want to take a nap.

Negative response
Jason, if you don't take a nap, you can't have a snack today.

Positive response from the video
Jason, it's nap time and here's your mat. I need you to lie down and be quiet. You don't have to go to sleep. Lie down and look at this book.

Another positive response

_____

_____

Scenario 7

Three boys and the caregiver sit at a table playing with plastic animals. Julie stands nearby and refuses to join them.

Negative response
What's your problem, Julie? Are you afraid of the boys?

Positive response from the video
Julie, this is your place. Come and join us. Remember the giraffe we saw at the zoo? Come and try to find a giraffe in this pile of animals that matches your paper cutout.

Another positive response

_____

_____

Activity 5
Learning About Discipline

Learning Objectives

After you have finished this activity, you will be able to do the following:

1. Explain the differences between discipline and punishment
2. Tell how to promote good behavior by using discipline, not punishment
3. Tell about self-discipline and how you can encourage children to develop self-discipline
4. List the 3 intervention techniques to use when a child misbehaves
5. Tell ways you can use the program and the child care setting to encourage children's good behavior

Lessons

- You must use good communication techniques when you discipline children.
- Self-discipline is the ability of children to control their own behavior. Children gradually learn that when they practice self-discipline, they have more control over what happens. They can expect positive results when they behave well. You can help children make this connection by letting children know that their everyday good behavior pleases you.
- The foundations of self-discipline are trust and consistency. Infants and children who trust that their needs will be met do not misbehave as often. They grow into children who know that if they use self-discipline and behave well, their behavior will have positive results.
- You must behave with children and talk to and listen to children in ways that help children learn self-discipline. The ways include the following:

  1. Understand how children are likely to behave at various ages and stages of development. For example, at certain ages children may say *no* alot because they want to be independent. Knowing why children behave as they do is an important step in deciding how to help children grow and learn.
  2. Listen patiently to children's ideas and feelings, or try to figure out what children's behavior might mean if the children are too young to talk.
  3. Help children find the words that best express their feelings.
  4. Do not take sides in disputes between children. Help children find their own best solutions.
  5. Use every situation to help children learn and develop in a positive way.
  6. Encourage children to use words, not fists, to solve problems.
  7. Deal with aggressive behavior as soon as it happens.

- You should know the differences between discipline and punishment.
  Discipline means using guidance and teaching techniques that promote good behavior and discourage bad behavior. Discipline is not the same as punishment.
  Punishment means using words or actions that hurt children. Punishment may stop bad behavior for a short time, but it does not teach children the right way to act. Punishment causes pain and can be very bad for a child.

- You will join a discussion group to talk about one of the topics listed on the flip chart and below. Later during the class discussion, you may take notes under each discussion topic.

Discussion Topic 1: Describe discipline and how to achieve it.

_____

_____

_____

_____

_____

_____

_____

_____

_____

_____

Discussion Topic 2: What is self-discipline?

_____

_____

_____

_____

_____

_____

_____

_____

_____

_____

Discussion Topic 3: How can the caregiver encourage the child to develop self-discipline?

_____

_____

_____

_____

_____

_____

_____

_____

_____

_____

Discussion Topic 4: How can the caregiver use the child care setting and its program to achieve good discipline?

_____

_____

_____

_____

_____

_____

_____

_____

_____

_____

***Discussion Topic 5: How should the caregiver intervene
when a child misbehaves?***

_____

_____

_____

_____

_____

_____

_____

_____

_____

_____

Activity 6
Management Plans: Child Behavior

Learning Objectives

After you finish this activity, you will be able to do the following:
1. List some rules to help children learn good behavior
2. Tell why children should share in making rules and solving problems

Lessons

- Use these guidelines to help children learn good behavior.

Behavior Guidelines
1. Set up a daily routine so children know what to expect. But be flexible.
2. Make sure children understand any special rules of your child care setting.

3. Give a 5-minute warning before cleanup, nap time, or any other change in activity. This allows time for children to change easily from one activity to the next.

4. Encourage preschoolers to take turns, and introduce them to the concept of sharing. This helps them to develop self-discipline. (Infants and toddlers are too immature to understand the concept of sharing.)

5. Encourage children's positive behavior by giving them your full attention and enthusiasm. Always behave the way you would want children to behave.

- Children and the caregiver share the child care setting. They should also share in making rules and solving problems. This encourages understanding and future cooperation and teaches children self-discipline. Children must learn to understand that rules help people get along with each other. Children benefit from solving problems because it helps them understand which are the correct ways to behave.

- You will work with a small group to develop a management plan based on the scenarios on page F-18. Your instructor will assign you a scenario. Then you will write a plan on the Management Plan Worksheet on page F-19. Fill in the blanks under the headings "What You Need to Know" and "What You Need to Do." Use your common sense and experience when you develop your plan.

Management Plans Scenarios

Scenario 1
Girl Bites Boy

Alice bites Chris, who runs to tell the caregiver about what happened. The caregiver comforts Chris and tells Alice that biting hurts.

Scenario 2
Two Boys Argue About a Trike

Tyrone and Jonathan both want to ride the tricycle. It is the only trike the right size for either boy that isn't already being used.

Scenario 3
Girl Throwing Books

Michelle is angry and is taking books from a shelf and throwing them across the room.

Scenario 4
Girl Pounds the Table

Elizabeth is having a temper tantrum. She is crumpling up the pretty drawing that she just finished and is pounding the table in an obvious effort to get the caregiver's attention.

Scenario 5
Girl Refuses Nap

Jennifer is coloring. When the caregiver asks her to take a nap, she refuses.

Scenario 6
Boy Spills Juice

Three-year-old Bruce doesn't like his juice and pours the juice on the floor.

Management Plan Worksheet

Scenario Number _____ **Title** _____

_____

_____

_____

_____

What You Need to Know

_____

_____

_____

_____

_____

What You Need to Do

_____

_____

_____

_____

_____

_____

_____

_____

_____

Management Plans

Scenario 1
Girl Bites Boy

Alice bites Chris, who runs to tell the caregiver about what happened. The caregiver comforts Chris and tells Alice that biting hurts.

What You Need to Know
- Biting is dangerous. It can lead to infection if the skin is broken.
- Biting is frightening to both children involved. The child who is bitten has been hurt; the child who bites may feel out of control and afraid of his or her own anger.
- Mild biting is developmentally appropriate for toddlers and is not considered bad behavior. The caregiver should still intervene when mild biting occurs to prevent it from developing into aggressive biting. Aggressive biting should be treated as a serious problem.

What You Need to Do
- Stay calm.
- Separate the children.
- Comfort the hurt child and find out if he or she needs first aid. Bites that break the skin need to be washed with soap and water and rinsed thoroughly.
- Tell the child who bites that biting is bad, can be dangerous, and is against the rules.
- Tell the child who bites that you don't want him or her to hurt anyone and that biting will not be tolerated.
- Tell both children's parents about the incident.
- Fill out an injury report form for the child care setting's records and one for the injured child's file.

Scenario 2
Two Boys Argue About a Trike

Tyrone and Jonathan both want to ride the tricycle. It is the only trike the right size for either boy that isn't already being used.

What You Need to Know
- Children sometimes argue.
- The caregiver can stop arguments by distracting the children with alternate games or plans.
- Arguing is a way to establish power and control.

What You Need to Do
- Stop the argument with simple, firm words.
- Offer an alternative toy or activity.
- Remind the children about taking turns and/or sharing toys.

Scenario 3
Girl Throws Books

Michelle is angry and is taking books from a shelf and throwing them across the room.

What You Need to Know
- Children can act out their anger in ways that can hurt them.
- Children can hurt others when they are angry.
- Children can damage property when they are angry.
- The caregiver must assess the situation. Can the child hurt himself or herself, or hurt others? Or can you ignore the acting out?

What You Need to Do
- Stop the child from hurting himself or herself.
- Explain to the child that while children can get angry with each other, they must use words rather than force to solve their differences or problems.
- Suggest a safe alternative, such as "If you are still angry, tell me how you are feeling. Then maybe we can go outside so you can play on the swings for awhile."

Management Plans

Scenario 4
Girl Pounds the Table

Elizabeth is having a temper tantrum. She is crumpling up the pretty drawing she just finished and is pounding on the table in an obvious effort to get the caregiver's attention.

What You Need to Know
- Children can act out their anger in ways that can hurt them.
- Children can hurt others when they are angry.
- The caregiver must assess the situation. Can the child hurt himself or herself, or hurt others? Or can the caregiver ignore the acting out?
- Paying attention to bad behavior only reinforces it.

What You Need to Do
- Look to see if the child is hurting himself or herself.
- If the child is not hurting himself or herself, the caregiver can ignore his bad behavior.
- Tell the parent if the child acts out his or her anger often during the day. The parent will need to know in case this is a sign of a deeper problem.

Scenario 5
Girl Refuses Nap

Jennifer is coloring. When the caregiver asks her to take a nap, she refuses.

What You Need to Know
- Children may not want to stop playing to take a nap.
- Some children may have a special problem that may make them restless and unable to relax easily.

What You Need to Do
- Offer the child a quiet activity he or she can do lying down.
- Speak with the child's parents if the child always refuses to rest. There may be a problem that needs attention.

Scenario 6
Boy Spills Juice

Three-year-old Bruce doesn't like his juice and pours the juice on the floor.

What You Need to Know
- People may slip on spilled juice, and fall and hurt themselves.
- Three-year-olds can be very forceful in letting you know what they like and don't like.
- The child may be angry or upset.

What You Need to Do
- Wipe up the spill before anyone is injured. If possible, get the child to help.
- Explain to the child that it is OK not to like things, but he or she should talk about it, not act on the dislike.
- Explain that someone could slip on the spilled juice and be hurt.

Activity 7
Communicating With Parents

After you finish this activity, you will be able to do the following:
1. Tell why you must communicate well with the parent
2. Tell ways for you and the parent to share information
3. Tell how to be supportive to parents
4. Tell how to use words, gestures, and tone of voice to communicate effectively with parents

Lessons

- The parent is, and should be, the most important person in a child's life. You should help support that relationship. You can help parents become more effective in their role and can teach parents about positive ways to work with children. But you also play a valuable role in the child's life.
- There are several ways you can share information with parents. These include the following:
  - Written policies about the child care program given to parents at the time of registration
  - Newsletters and bulletins
  - Telephone calls
  - Special appointments for the parent to visit the child care setting or for you to visit the child's home
  - Informal tours or talks when the parent picks up his or her child
  - Daily chats or informal notes to report good news or problems
  - A notebook for each child so that parents and you can record facts and information
- Use the rules below to communicate well with parents.

Communicating With Parents

1. Speak politely and caringly. Listen patiently and respectfully. This establishes a caregiver-parent relationship of warmth and trust.
2. Share information about the child in a factual, calm way.
3. Allow parents to express their concerns about their children.
4. Discuss and settle problems together, without showing strong, negative emotions.
5. Speak respectfully about a parent's religious, social, political, cultural, and educational values.

Activity 8
Management Plans: Dealing With Parents

Learning Objectives

After finishing this activity, you will be able to do the following:
1. Explain why you must communicate well with the parent
2. Tell ways for you and the parent to share information effectively
3. Tell how to support a parent's role with the child

Lesson

- You will work with a small group to develop a management plan based on a scenario your instructor will assign you. Then you will write a plan in the spaces on the Management Plan Worksheet on page F-26. Fill in the blanks under the headings "What You Need to Know" and "What You Need to Do." Use your common sense and experience when you develop your plan. Then each person in your group will select a role from the names that appear in boldface type in your group's scenario. You will perform the scenario and discuss your management plan with the class.

Management Plans Scenarios

Scenario 1
Tardy Mother

One mother, **Vivian**, often comes half-an-hour late to pick up her 4-year-old daughter, **Ashley**. She never makes excuses and she never apologizes to the caregiver, **Melanie**. She also yells at her daughter to hurry up because she is in a hurry. Today, she arrives late again to pick up Ashley, who is sick and needs to see a doctor. Vivian's husband, **Clark**, is in the car, honking and shouting.

Scenario 2
Angry Father

An angry father, **Anthony**, comes to the child care setting at noon. He demands that the caregiver, **Cleo**, discuss immediately with him a problem with 2-year-old **Augustus** and the child's bad behavior and language. Another child, **Julian**, is crying because he is hungry.

Scenario 3
Custody Problems

Christopher and **Susan** Farwell have recently separated. They argue over child care and custody, particularly over who is to pick up their 5-year-old son, **Michael**. Often they both have arrived at pickup time. This causes their son to be anxious every afternoon. One Friday night, Susan arrives and tells the caregiver, **Elana**, that the father will not be picking up the child anymore. At that moment, Christopher arrives.

Scenario 4
Toilet-Training Problems

Parents **Elizabeth** and **Henry** arrive at the child care setting to find their daughter, 3½-year-old **Ann**, in wet pants. They tell the caregiver, **Robin**, that their daughter never wets her pants at home and demand to know why she wets her pants so often at the child care setting. They are very angry. Elizabeth insists on speaking to the director, Mrs. Boleyn, right away about this matter.

Scenario 5
Biting Child

One-and-a-half-year-old **Eleanor** bites a playmate, 11-month-old Franklin, leaving a red mark, but not breaking the skin. The caregiver, **Winston**, must explain to Eleanor's mother, **Mrs. Delano**, and to Franklin's mother, **Mrs. Spencer**, what happened when the mothers pick up their children.

Management Plan Worksheet

Scenario Number _____ **Title** _____

_____

_____

_____

_____

What You Need to Know

_____

_____

_____

_____

_____

What You Need to Do

_____

_____

_____

_____

_____

_____

_____

_____

_____

_____

Management Plans

Scenario 1
Tardy Mother

One mother, **Vivian**, often comes half-an-hour late to pick up her 4-year-old daughter, **Ashley**. She never makes excuses and she never apologizes to the caregiver, **Melanie**. She also yells at her daughter to hurry up because she is in a hurry. Today, she arrives late again to pick up Ashley, who is sick and needs to see a doctor. Vivian's husband, **Clark**, is in the car, honking and shouting.

What You Need to Know
- A parent can have last-minute, on-the-job time problems that cause delays in picking up the child.
- A parent can run into traffic jams or have car problems, scheduling mix-ups, or medical appointments, etc., that cause delays in picking up the child.
- A parent worries about how to care for an ill child and how to manage job responsibilities at the same time.
- A parent should have a regular schedule for picking up the child.
- The caregiver should be flexible, but must also establish a schedule and rules for proper pickup times.
- A child can get upset if his or her parent is late.

What You Need to Do
- Reassure the child that his or her parent is coming. Offer the child a quiet activity.
- Wait with the child for the parent, if possible. Help the child feel comfortable.
- Stay calm.
- Have the child and his or her belongings ready to leave as soon as the parent arrives. This helps out the parent.
- Greet the parent in a friendly way. Never be rude or critical. Explain the situation and share any necessary information.

- Try to understand the parent's position and his or her stress and worry.
- Explain the rules to all parents.
- Remind the parent who is frequently late of the rules for pickup times; tell the parent that he or she must abide by the rules.

Scenario 2
Angry Father

An angry father, **Anthony**, comes to the child care setting at noon. He demands that the caregiver, **Cleo**, discuss immediately with him a problem with 2-year-old **Augustus** and the child's bad behavior and language. Another child, **Julian**, is crying because he is hungry.

What You Need to Know
- A parent's main concern is the welfare of the child.
- The caregiver must be flexible, but should not leave the children alone in order to speak with a parent during regular hours.
- Problems can best be discussed when everyone is calm and objective.
- Young children do not need to be a part of a discussion between the caregiver and the parent.

What You Need to Do
- Stay calm and courteous. Explain that you cannot leave the children alone.
- Ask the parent to tell you a convenient time when he or she can return for a private meeting with you.
- Assure the parent you understand that his or her concern is serious and you will be happy to discuss it or refer the parent to an expert, if necessary.
- Suggest that the parent meet with the director, if appropriate.

Management Plans

Scenario 3
Custody Problems

Christopher and **Susan** Farwell have recently separated. They argue over child care and custody, particularly over who is to pick up their 5-year-old son, **Michael**. Often they both have arrived at pickup time. This causes their son to be anxious every afternoon. One Friday night, Susan arrives and tells the caregiver, **Elana**, that the father will not be picking up the child anymore. At that moment, Christopher arrives.

What You Need to Know
- Children need to know that they can count on the adults in their life.
- Children may be very unhappy by the problems in their home life, particularly when parents separate and are angry with each other.
- The caregiver may be the most stable person for a child in times of crises in a child's life.

What You Need to Do
- Ask to talk privately with the parents, either together or separately. Explain that you are concerned that the uncertainty is causing Michael a lot of anxiety, especially close to pickup time.
- Talk about the child's welfare, not about any marital problems or parental disagreements.
- Ask the parents to give you a copy of their pickup schedule so that all people know whom to expect each evening. Ask the parents to keep you informed of any scheduling changes.
- Tell them that you understand how difficult the situation is for both parents.
- Ask that the parents inform you of any legal actions that affect custody and/or child visitation rights.

Scenario 4
Toilet-Training Problems

Parents **Elizabeth** and **Henry** arrive at the child care setting to find their daughter, 3½-year-old **Ann**, in wet pants. They tell the caregiver, **Robin**, that their daughter never wets her pants at home and demand to know why she wets her pants so often at the child care setting. They are both very angry. Elizabeth insists on speaking to the director, Mrs. Boleyn, right away about this matter.

What You Need to Know
- It is not unusual for a child this age to have lapses in toilet training; the parents may expect too much too soon.
- The parents' anxiety and pressure may make the child feel self-conscious.
- Parents may be overly-concerned about a child's developmental abilities.
- Lapses in toilet training may be caused by physical problems.

What You Need to Do
- Acknowledge the parents' concern.
- Reassure them that each child learns proper toilet habits at a different rate and at a different age.
- Explain to the parents that some children may have lapses in toilet training while they are adjusting to a new environment, even though they don't wet their pants at home.
- Explain to the mother that the child may feel embarrassed about her lack of control in front of the other children.
- Pay special attention to the child and encourage her to learn proper toilet habits at her own pace.
- If the problem continues, suggest that the parents speak to the child's doctor about it.

Management Plans

Scenario 5
Biting Child

One-and-a-half-year-old **Eleanor** bites a play-mate, 11-month-old Franklin, leaving a red mark, but not breaking the skin. The caregiver, **Winston,** must explain to Eleanor's mother, **Mrs. Delano**, and to Franklin's mother, **Mrs. Spencer**, what happened when the mothers pick up their children.

What You Need to Know
- The child may have bitten many times for no apparent reason.
- Sometimes children express their anger by biting.

What You Need to Do
- Explain to both mothers that children may bite when they are angry.
- Talk with Eleanor's mother about good ways for Eleanor to express her anger.
- Figure out ways to discipline, not punish, Eleanor. Or change the situation so that biting does not recur.
- Reassure Franklin's mother that you will try to prevent Eleanor from biting Franklin again.
- Fill out an injury report form to give to both sets of parents.

Activity 9
Test and Unit Evaluation

Objective

After you have finished this activity, you will be able to do the following:
1. Complete the test

Lessons

- The test that the instructor will give you has 25 questions about what you learned in this class. Answer the questions on the answer sheet. You must score 80 percent or higher (or answer 20 or more questions correctly) to pass this unit.
- Your instructor will also give you a unit evaluation sheet. Please tell us what you thought of this unit by filling out this sheet and returning it to the instructor.
- Thank you for your participation in the American Red Cross Child Care Course. By taking all of the units of the Child Care Course, you are showing your commitment to giving the best possible child care. Now that you understand the information and skills presented, you will be able to put your caring and concern for children into action.

American Red Cross Child Care Course: Recognizing and Reporting Child Abuse

Contents

About the Recognizing and Reporting Child Abuse Unit

Caregivers need to know about child abuse because it is a wide-spread problem that exists at all levels of society. The National Committee for Prevention of Child Abuse (NCPCA) estimates that more than a million cases of suspected child abuse are reported and that more than 1,200 children die as the result of abuse each year. For those who survive, the hurt they have suffered influences their entire life. According to the American Academy of Pediatrics, many children who are abused may, as adults, be unhappy, have low self-esteem, and have little success at work or in relationships. They may themselves become abusive parents or engage in other socially deviant behavior in adolescence and adulthood.

According to the NCPCA, the caregiver can play an important role in preventing child abuse by supporting parents in their parental role and by encouraging quality parenting. You can also readily intervene on a child's behalf and can help improve the quality of a child's life by recognizing and reporting the signs of child abuse and neglect.

This unit will teach you which community resources to use to help prevent child abuse and neglect and how to report suspected cases of child abuse accurately. You can help prevent child abuse and neglect. You can help make a child's life happier and more secure.

The information for the activities in the Recognizing and Report-ing Child Abuse unit comes from material supplied by the NCPCA. (The appendixes were developed separately.)

What You Will Learn

This unit will teach you—
1. What child abuse is.
2. What signs of child abuse to look for.
3. Why child abuse happens.
4. Which adults are likely to abuse children.
5. Which authorities to contact about suspected abuse.
6. How to report a suspected case of abuse.
7. Which community resources to use to help prevent child abuse.

Further Information

For further information about child abuse, write the National Committee for Prevention of Child Abuse, 332 South Michigan Ave., Suite 1600, Chicago, IL 60604; and the American Academy of Pediatrics, P.O. Box 927, Elk Grove Village, IL 60009-0927.

Activity 1
Orientation

Objective

After you have finished this activity, you will be able to do the following:
1. Tell the unit requirements

Lessons

- Your instructor will discuss the unit with you and what you must do to pass it. The unit requirements are—
  - Satisfactory performance on the test—80 percent or higher (or 20 correct answers).
  - Attendance of the class.
- You will review the contents of the workbook.

Recognizing and Reporting Child Abuse Unit Agenda

Activity	Topic
1	Orientation
2	Introductions
3	General Information About Child Abuse
4	About Emotional Maltreatment
5	About Physical Abuse and Neglect
Break	
6	About Sexual Abuse
7	Getting Community Help
8	Calling for Help: Role-Playing
9	Test and Unit Evaluation

Activity 2
Introductions

Objectives

After you have finished this activity, you will be able to do the following:
1. Use the All About You sheet to tell the group about yourself
2. Tell why you are taking this unit

Lesson

• Fill out the All About You sheet. The sheet is on the next page.

All About You

Fill in the blanks.

1. What is your name? _____

2. Where do you work? _____

3. What is your job there? _____

4. How old are the children in your group? _____

5. Why are you taking this unit? _____

6. What do you hope to learn? _____

_____

_____

Activity 3
General Information About Child Abuse

Learning Objectives

After you have finished this activity, you will be able to do the following:
1. Tell what child abuse is
2. Recognize some general signs of child abuse
3. Tell why child abuse happens
4. Explain who child abusers may be

Lessons

- *Child abuse* means an injury or a pattern of injuries that happens to a child and that is not an accident. According to the NCPCA, child abuse is damage to a child for which there is no logical reason or explanation.
- Child abuse includes the following categories:
    1. Emotional maltreatment—Criticisms, mean remarks, insults, or teasing. Also, it can mean the parent gives little or no love, guidance, care, or support to the child, or the parent expects the child to do better than the child is able to do.
    2. Physical abuse—Beatings, burns, strangulation, bites, or other signs of physical harm.
    3. Physical neglect—The parent does not provide proper or enough food, clothing, shelter, or medical care.
    4. Sexual abuse—The sexual use of a child for an adult's or other person's pleasure.
- An abused child may show some of the following signs:
    1. The child acts strangely or changes behavior suddenly.
    2. The child keeps to himself or herself.
    3. The child acts unfriendly or tough.
    4. The child is afraid to go home.
    5. The child is suspicious or watchful of others, as if afraid of harm.

- Child abuse can happen for any of the following reasons:
    1. The abusing adult was abused as a child. Not all abused children grow up to be abusive parents, but many do. Abusive parenting is all they have known.
    2. The abusing adult dislikes himself or herself.
    3. The abusing adult cannot meet his or her own needs.
    4. The abusing adult is unwilling or unable to seek professional help.
    5. The abusing adult has unrealistic expectations of a child's developmental levels or stages.
    6. The abusing adult believes a parent can treat a child as he or she pleases, even if that includes abuse.
    7. The abusing adult accepts violence as a normal way to deal with life.
    8. The abusing adult thinks of the child as unappealing or somehow different from other children or thinks that the child has special needs. Perhaps the child's conduct or traits remind the abuser about something he or she does not like about his or her own childhood self.
    9. The abusing adult finds the child particularly difficult to care for.
    10. The abusing adult is not coping with stressful circumstances in his or her life.
- People who abuse children are usually ordinary people trapped in stressful lives they cannot seem to control. The abuser can be anyone, including a friend, a neighbor, a relative, or a caregiver. One caregiver may see another caregiver abusing a child.

    The abuser can be of any age and of either sex. Contrary to a popular belief, child abuse does not happen only to minorities or to the poor. Child abusers can come from any economic, racial, ethnic, or religious group.

    Some categories of people, however, seem more likely to abuse children. For example, those with serious money problems or those with seriously troubled marriages may be suffering unusual stress. Stress, or a combination of other factors, may trigger child abuse. A caregiver who is under stress may also be likely to abuse a child.
- Parents who abuse their children usually love their children, but in times of stress or trouble strike out at those who are closest—their children. In most cases, however, with outside help, abusive parents can learn to deal with their problems and to provide a safe environment for their children.
- For further information, turn to Appendix A, Signs of Child Abuse.

Activity 4
About Emotional Maltreatment

Learning Objectives

After you have finished this activity, you will be able to do the following:
1. Tell what emotional (psychological) maltreatment is
2. Tell why emotional maltreatment happens
3. Recognize some signs of emotional maltreatment

Lessons

- *Emotional maltreatment* means using words that hurt children. According to the NCPCA, it also means acting in ways that tell a child that he or she is not loved, not wanted, and not able to do well. This makes a child feel bad about himself or herself and causes the child to misbehave. Emotional maltreatment may occur with or without physical abuse.
- There are 5 forms of emotional maltreatment:
  1. Rejecting—Parents do not accept the child for himself or herself.
  2. Ignoring—Parents do not pay attention to the child and his or her feelings.
  3. Terrorizing—Parents use mean words or actions that make the child afraid.

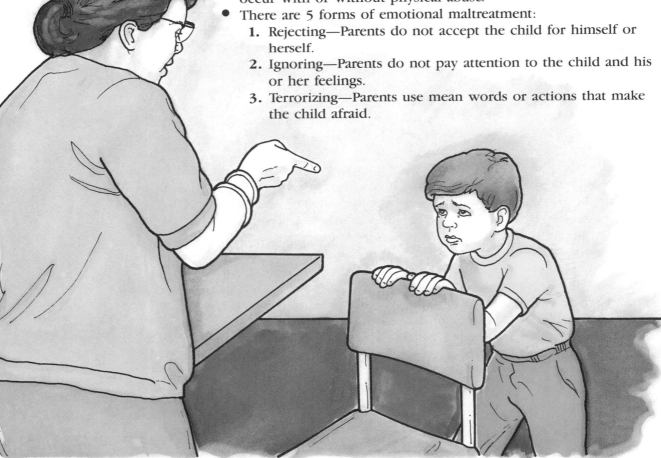

4. Isolating—Parents keep the child from having normal relationships.
5. Corrupting—Parents teach the child abnormal, immoral, or wrong behavior. Or the parents vividly describe sexual acts in front of the child.

- Parents who emotionally maltreat their children may belong to one of the following categories:
    1. The parents are not able to understand or to deal with children.
    2. The parents are disturbed and they harm their children emotionally on purpose.
    3. The parents have wrong ideas about what a child needs to grow up properly.
    4. The parents lead lives that are out of control.
    5. The parents have too much or too little control over their emotions.

Activity 5
About Physical Abuse and Neglect

Learning Objectives

After you have finished this activity, you will be able to do the following:
1. Tell about physical abuse and why it happens
2. Recognize the signs of physical abuse
3. Tell about physical neglect and why it happens
4. Recognize the signs of physical neglect

Lessons

- *Physical abuse* means injuries that an adult does to a child on purpose. According to the NCPCA, these injuries may include severe beatings, burns, human bites, strangulation, or burning with hot water. Physical abuse usually does not mean just one attack on a child, but instead, a series of attacks that happen over a certain time period.

  You may suspect physical abuse if the child has one or several of the following conditons:
  1. Bruises, broken bones, cuts, puncture marks, swollen areas, missing hair, or bite or burn marks.
  2. Frequent signs of minor or major injuries.
  3. Different injuries in varying stages of healing.
  4. Odd or hard-to-believe explanations for the child's injuries. For example, the child may explain a bruised leg by saying that his mother broke her toe on his leg when she accidentally kicked him.
  5. Frequent tardiness or absences.
  6. Overdue, unsuitable, or nonexistent treatment for injuries.
- The child who is physically abused usually acts one of the following 2 ways:
  1. The child is compliant (will do whatever is asked), shy, withdrawn, passive, and uncommunicative (quiet or reserved).
  2. The child is nervous, overactive, angry, and destructive.
- Parents who physically abuse their children may feel worthless, may be unable to trust others, may have a very bad marriage, or may have had a very unhappy childhood.

- *Physical neglect* happens to a child when the parents do not or cannot give the child the basic care or the basic items that the child needs to live, such as food, clothing, shelter, or medical care. Children who are physically neglected suffer from what their parents *do not do* to or for them. Physical neglect can happen in both poor and rich families.
- The child who is physically neglected is likely to act in certain of the following ways:
    1. The child worries that he or she will suffer injury or serious harm.
    2. The child shows little energy or is too active.
    3. The child may be hungry or dirty or wear dirty clothes.
    4. The child shows a change in behavior.

In addition, the physically neglected child may show one or more of the following traits:
- The child cannot concentrate or play.
- The child has trouble learning.
- The child often seeks attention.

Note: These traits, when found alone, don't necessarily mean that a child is physically neglected. But when many of these traits are present together, or when there is a pattern, the possibility of physical neglect should be considered.
- Parents who neglect their children may not have had enough love and attention themselves and they may not be very interested in their children. Or they cannot give proper physical care to them.

Activity 6
About Sexual Abuse

Learning Objectives

After you have finished this activity, you will be able to do the following:
1. Tell about sexual abuse and why it happens
2. Recognize signs of sexual abuse

Lessons

- *Sexual abuse* means the sexual use of a child for an adult's or other person's pleasure. Adults, adolescents, or children who sexually abuse children most likely have been abused themselves and have never received treatment of any kind.

    The abuser always uses either physical or emotional force on the child. The force may be very hard to detect. Sexual abuse includes both touching and nontouching of the child's body. Sexual abuse is not the same thing as normal physical affection between an adult and a child. Responsible people limit their physical contact with a child.

    Sexual abuse is never the child's fault; it is always the responsibility of the abuser.
- Sexual abuse can include the following activities:
    1. Exhibitionism—An adult exposes his or her genitals to a child.
    2. Voyeurism—An adult watches a child undress, bathe, or use the bathroom at times when this watching is not needed.
    3. Kissing—An adult gives a long or intimate kiss to a child.
    4. Fondling—An adult touches, strokes, or rubs a child's genitals, or has the child do it to himself or herself.
    5. Anal, vaginal, or oral intercourse.
    6. Pornography—An adult shows a child materials that show sexual acts between a child and an adult, between adults, or between children, or an adult uses a child to produce such material.

- The general signs of sexual abuse in a child include, but are not limited to, the following:
  1. Physical signs—Pain in or injury to the mouth or the genital area; irritated, reddened, or itching genitals; urinary infections or difficulty with urination; or unusual odors.
  2. Behavior changes—Fear of a person or of certain places; sudden interest in the genitals of others; unsuitable sexual activity for the child's age, such as French kissing; or acting out of sexual behavior with toys or animals. Children who have been sexually abused may also have the more general characteristics of clinging, being anxious or irritable, or returning to infantile behavior.

     According to the NCPCA, "There are several clues to look for when considering the possibility of sexual child abuse. One sign alone may not be a positive indication; if a number are present, it is wise to consider the possibility of sexual child abuse."
  3. The abuser is usually someone the child knows and trusts. When the abuser is a family member, the sexual abuse is known as *incest*. In rare cases, the abuser may be a brother or sister or a playmate who is, most likely, a victim of child abuse. A child may be sexually abused by anyone.

Activity 7
Getting Community Help

Learning Objective

After you have finished this activity, you will be able to do the following:

1. Tell when and where to report child abuse

Note: Your instructor will use either Activity 7 or Activity 8, but not both.

Lessons

- All states have laws against child abuse. These laws say that people who work with children must report suspected cases of child abuse. You do not need to have proof that abuse has happened, only a reasonable cause to believe it happened. You should also report cases in which you think abuse may happen in the future. You cannot stop or prevent child abuse unless you report it.

- Every state and many communities have at least one agency, such as the Department of Social Services, the Department of Children and Family Services, or Child Protective Services (CPS), to which you can make your report.
- The goals of reporting child abuse include the following:
  - To identify the child
  - To guard the child's safety
  - To determine if abuse or neglect is present
  - To stop the abuse and neglect
  - To offer appropriate resources and treatment to the child and the family
  - To strengthen the family, if possible

  The goal of reporting should be to protect children, not to punish abusers.
- Each child care setting should have established procedures for reporting suspected child abuse. The procedures should do the following:
  - State how and to whom reports of suspected child abuse are to be made
  - Provide for the confidential handling of the report
  - Specify whether, how, and by whom parents will be notified that the report has been filed
- You may be afraid to report child abuse because you do not wish to get involved or you are afraid of being sued. But when you make a report in good faith, you are immune from any civil or criminal liability or penalty, even if you make a mistake. In this instance, *good faith* means that you honestly believe that the abuse has occurred or the potential for abuse exists and that a prudent and reasonable person in the same position as you would also honestly believe that the abuse has occurred or that the potential for abuse exists. You *will* get into trouble if you do *not* report child abuse. You may not have to identify yourself when you make a report.
- For information on finding out how to get help for families that have special problems, turn to Appendix B, Community Resources.
- You can help parents by teaching them about how children normally grow and act. You can teach parents positive ways to deal with children. You can support parents and refer them to groups such as Parents Anonymous. With proper training, you can also develop the skills to identify children and adults at risk before abuse occurs.

Activity 8
Calling for Help: Role-Playing

Learning Objectives

After you have finished this activity, you will be able to do the following:

1. Call the local reporting agency and be prepared to ask and answer the correct questions about suspected child abuse
2. State clearly that the goal of reporting child abuse is to protect children, not to punish abusers

Note: Your instructor will use either Activity 7 or Activity 8, but not both.

Lessons

- All states have laws against child abuse. These laws say that people who work with children must report suspected cases of child abuse. You do not need to have proof that abuse has happened, only a reasonable cause to believe it happened. You should also report cases in which you think abuse may happen in the future. You cannot stop or prevent child abuse unless you report it.
- Every state and many communities have at least one agency, such as the Department of Social Services, the Department of Children and Family Services, or Child Protective Services (CPS), to which you can make your report.
- The goals of reporting child abuse include the following:
  - To identify the child
  - To guard the child's safety
  - To determine if abuse or neglect is present
  - To stop the abuse and neglect
  - To offer appropriate resources and treatment to the child and the family
  - To strengthen the family, if possible

  The goal of reporting should be to protect children, not to punish abusers.
- Each child care setting should have established procedures for reporting suspected child abuse. The procedures should do the following:
  - State how and to whom reports of suspected child abuse are to be made
  - Provide for the confidential handling of the report
  - Specify whether, how, and by whom parents will be notified that the report has been filed
- You may be afraid to report child abuse because you do not wish to get involved or you are afraid of being sued. But when you make a report in good faith, you are immune from any civil or criminal liability or penalty, even if you make a mistake. In this instance, *good faith* means that you honestly believe that the abuse has occurred or the potential for abuse exists and that a prudent and reasonable person in the same position as you would also honestly believe that the abuse has occurred or that the potential for abuse exists. You *will* get into trouble if you do *not* report child abuse. You may not have to identify yourself when you make a report.
- Turn to the Calling for Help Scenarios on page G-19. You will work with a partner to act out a role as a reporter of the child abuse described in one of the scenarios or as a person at the Child Protective Services (CPS) who takes the report. Your instructor will assign you a scenario. The person acting as the CPS representative should use the questions on page G-20 as a guide. Then you will discuss the scenario.

- During the discussion, you will answer the following questions:
  1. How did you feel about making the call to report abuse (reporter)?
  2. How did you feel about the responses you heard (CPS representative)?
  3. Did you keep in mind that the goal of the call is to help the child, not to punish the abuser?
- For further information, turn to Appendix C, What Happens When You Call.

Calling For Help Scenarios

Scenario 1 (Emotional abuse)

Sheila is 4 years old. Each evening when her mother comes to pick her up from child care, Sheila becomes nervous and says that she is not ready to go home. When Sheila's mother arrives, she just stands near the door and stares at Sheila. Sheila knows to go to the door to leave. This happens almost automatically. The mother does not speak to Sheila or the caregiver, and Sheila stops speaking abruptly when the mother arrives.

Scenario 2 (Physical abuse)

Douglas is 4 years old. The caregiver notices that when the children play "house," Douglas always wants to be the daddy. Daddy beats the dolls and throws them around. When the mommy asks him to stop, Douglas tells her, "Shut up, or you'll get it, too." One day while playing house, Douglas rolls up his shirt sleeves to wash up for dinner. His caregiver notices black, blue, and yellow bruises on Douglas's arms. There is also a big, red welt around his wrist.

Scenario 3 (Physical abuse)

Lisa is 3 years old. One Monday morning Lisa's caregiver notices that Lisa has small patches of hair missing from her scalp and that there are areas of redness on her scalp. This is the third time in 2 months this has happened.

Scenario 4 (Physical neglect)

Tony comes to child care each day dressed only in a T-shirt and the same pair of light cotton slacks. The weather is getting cold, and the caregiver has tried to talk to Tony's mother about dressing him properly so that he can play outside with the other children—but the mother is always too busy to talk. Tony also seems hungry and is small for his age.

Scenario 5 (Sexual abuse)

When the caregiver changes Kristy's diaper, she finds a small amount of blood on the inside of the diaper. While cleaning and checking Kristy, the caregiver notices that Kristy's genital area (vagina) is raw and swollen and that she has bruises on her inner thighs.

Scenario 6 (Emotional abuse)

When Bobby's father picks him up at the child care setting, the caregiver overhears the father calling the child such names as "dummy" and "ugly." She hears the father yelling at Bobby as they walk out to the car, telling him that he walks so slowly that he must be stupid and that he is useless and worthless. After the father puts Bobby into the car, the caregiver hears him telling Bobby not to move or say a word or the father will leave Bobby off at the nearest street corner and make him walk home.

Calling For Help Scenarios

Child Protective Services (CPS) Questions

1. Child's name _____

2. Child's address _____

3. Child's phone number _____

4. Name of child's parent _____

5. Name of suspected abuser _____

6. When you first noticed abuse _____

7. Description of signs of abuse _____

8. Name and phone number of caller _____

The caller may choose not to give his or her name.

Activity 9
Test and Unit Evaluation

Objective

After you have finished this activity, you will be able to do the following:

1. Complete the test

Lessons

- The test that the instructor will give you has 25 questions about what you learned in this class. Answer the questions on the answer sheet. You must score 80 percent or higher (or answer 20 or more questions correctly) to pass this unit.
- Your instructor will also give you a unit evaluation sheet. Please tell us what you thought of this unit by filling out this sheet and returning it to the instructor.
- Thank you for your participation in the American Red Cross Child Care Course. By taking all of the units of the Child Care Course, you are showing your commitment to giving the best possible child care. Now that you understand the information and skills presented, you will be able to put your caring and concern for children into action.

Appendixes

Signs of Child Abuse

Caregivers may suspect abuse when—
- The child shows sudden behavior changes or erratic behavior.
- The child becomes withdrawn.
- The child is hostile or extremely aggressive.
- The child fears going home at the end of the day.
- The child is suspicious or watchful of others' actions, as if fearing harm.

Caregivers may suspect emotional maltreatment if—
- The child cannot interact well socially, has very low self-esteem, or is listless, apathetic, or depressed and cannot respond to normal adult behavior.
- The child has a parent who treats the child in unusual or abnormal ways, such as refusing to care for or to talk to the child, treating the child as an object, keeping the child from normal social experiences, punishing the child for his or her normal behavior, and/or thinking or feeling in a consistently negative way about the child.

Caregivers may suspect physical abuse if—
- The child has bruises, broken bones, lacerations, puncture marks, swollen areas, missing hair, or bite or burn marks.
- The child has frequent signs of minor or major injuries.
- The child has different injuries in varying stages of healing.
- The parent or child gives odd or impossible explanations for the child's injuries.
- The child is frequently tardy or absent.
- The child receives overdue, unsuitable, or no treatment for injuries.

Caregivers may suspect physical neglect if—
- The child is anxious about his or her survival.
- The child lacks energy or is overactive.
- The child is unable to concentrate or to play.
- The child has trouble learning.
- The child often seeks attention.
- The child is hungry or dirty or wears dirty clothes.
- The child shows a change in behavior.

Caregivers may suspect sexual abuse if the child shows one or some of the following:
- Physical signs—Pain in or injury to the mouth or the genital area; irritated, reddened, or itching genitals; urinary infections or difficulty with urination; or unusual odors.
- Behavior changes—Fear of a person or of certain places; clinging, anxiety, or irritability; sudden interest in the genitals of others; unsuitable sexual activity for the child's age; acting out of sexual behavior with toys or animals; a return to infantile behavior.

Community Resources

Whenever a caregiver suspects that a child has been abused, or is about to be abused, he or she must report that suspicion to the correct agency or authority.

At other times, however, the caregiver may wish to refer parents to community resources that may be able to help them. Parents with job, money, or personal problems may be unable to care for their children properly and they may need help.

Public and private agencies and organizations in every community can help families who are in trouble. By referring parents to those who can assist them, you may be taking the first step towards eliminating actual or possible child abuse and neglect. The available help differs widely from community to community. The listings below should guide you to sources of help. You should also record the phone number of your local Child Abuse Hotline or similar emergency phone number.

_____

_____

_____

- **State, county, and municipal social services departments.**
  Government offices in your community can assist you in locating sources of specific kinds of help, even when they do not offer that help themselves. Government personnel can also help families to obtain food stamps or to find sources that donate food. They may offer help finding jobs; education and job training; and emergency shelter and food. Almost every community has its own child protective services agency and department of social services run by county or municipal personnel.

- **Private organizations.**
  Several private organizations offer services to help families in need. Sources include your Red Cross chapter; the local Mental Health Association; self-help groups such as Parents Anonymous and Alcoholics Anonymous; and youth organizations such as Big Brothers/Big Sisters and scouting groups.

- **Religious groups.**
  Houses of worship and religious organizations are a good source of help or referrals for families with emergency food, shelter, and counseling needs.

- **Local hospital and public library.**
  Hospital and library personnel are often familiar with community resources and can be a good source for referrals.

What Happens When You Call

Your local child protective services agency has simplified calling to report suspected child abuse. The caller's only job is to report the suspected abuse. The agency worker asks for the needed information and makes the decisions about which course of action to follow.

When you call the child protective services agency, a trained worker will answer the phone. He or she will ask the caller where the child lives and which child care program the child attends. The worker needs to determine whether the child is within that agency's jurisdiction or whether the child's case should be referred to another agency.

If the child is within the agency's jurisdiction, the worker will then decide which course of action to follow. Possible actions include the following:

- The worker comes to the child care setting to talk with the child and to document any signs of physical abuse.
- The worker talks further with the caller who reported the suspected abuse.
- The worker talks with the parent or parents.
- The worker talks with the child's health care professional.

The worker usually asks the caller several questions, which may include the following:
- The child's name
- The child's age
- The child's address
- The parents' names
- The parents' home and work phone numbers
- When the caller first noticed signs of abuse
- Whether the caller has noticed other incidents of abuse involving the same child
- The name, phone number, and address of caller (optional in some states)
- The hours during the day when the child is in the caller's care
- How many months or years the child has been in the caller's care

As a caregiver, you are required to report abuse as soon as you suspect it is happening. The worker needs, for example, to see the signs of physical abuse—that is, the bruises or cuts—and the worker needs to document the stages of healing. If you wait too long and the bruises or cuts go away, it is harder for the CPS worker to document a case of abuse.